HANDMADE

VANISHING CULTURES of EUROPE

AND THE NEAR EAST

BY

DREW & LOUISE LANGSNER

Harmony books

1974

Publisher: Bruce Harris

Editor: Linda Sunshine

Production Director: Murray Schwartz

Photography & Design: Drew Langsner

Phototypesetting: Dharma Press; Emeryville, Ca.

Halftones and negative preparation: Viking Litho; San Francisco, Ca.

Printing and bindery: Halliday Lithograph Corp.; Hanover, Mass.

MS. Readers: David Dann, Penn Jensen, Sophia Silver, Patrick Campbell, Liz Wilmot, Dennis McGinley

Help!: *Toward the One* and *Prophesy Pressworks*

Special Thanks: The Lama Foundation; San Cristobal, N.M.

CONTENTS

FIG. 1–Wash basin. Greece.

I. INTRODUCTION

"I remember little things, like the way we used to keep time in my parents' home. We did not need to measure time of day, but we needed to measure it for cooking. One method was to fill a special pot with water; the pot had a small hole in it, and it allowed water to escape, drop by drop. My mother would know to put in so much water to measure the time needed to cook such and such a meal. If we needed to be wakened up at a certain hour, my mother would light a stick of incense, of the right length. When it burned down to the end it would burn through a thread that held a stone above an old metal pot, and we would be awakened by the clanging and clattering as the stone fell. Otherwise we simply awoke when the cocks began crowing. During the day we knew the hour by the sun, at night by the stars. Our lives in Tibet were spent without haste, and without the strange force that presses people down here, so that they always seem to be doing one thing and wishing they were doing something else, as though they were being driven like animals. In Tibet I felt more free, and more alive, and although life may have been harder, living it was easier."[1]

WE found these lines by the light of a kerosene lamp during the winter of 1971–1972. At the time we were living in a small stone dwelling surrounded by a citrus grove; less than one hundred yards from the Aegean Sea. Thubten Jigme Norbu had been forced out of the Old World, and thrust into the technological age. We had departed from the New World to learn something from those who were left behind.

We lived up a crumbling stone staircase in a single room, formerly a kitchen, some 8 by 10 feet in dimension. On the ground floor were four rooms used for storage and animal shelters. We had one window, without glass, but fitted with board shutters. The fireplace was such that it would not heat even our small room. (This was the coldest winter in more than 30 years.) Our bed was straw. The roofing was tile, mortared over bamboo-lathing strips—aesthetic, and leaky. An early task was repairing the many drafts. There was no privy.

Why did we live that way? For one, this was a typical home for a part of humanity for many ages. But it was the first time we had lived for an extended period without electricity, running water, or neighborhood shopping center. We gathered firewood from the hills, learned to find wild greens for food, and did our cooking in the fireplace. We were searching out unfamous but significant roots of our heritage; sensing a highly developed attunement of humankind and nature in the simplicity of

---

[1] Copyright © 1968 by Thubten Jigme Norbu and Colin M. Turnbull in *Tibet: Its History, Religion and People.* Simon and Schuster, 1968.

pre-industrial life. We believed that learning from experience about other people's worlds would be helpful in developing our own.

During our travels we met people whose income was so small that we could hardly discern its source. Yet many times, country folk took us into their homes, and fed us meals that can only be described as wonderful. A Turkish village, literally made of mud, was cleaner than the residential districts of most American cities. Lack of waste is one factor. The Islamic teachings of order and personal hygiene are another.

The path of our travels might resemble a tangled piece of string superimposed over a map of Europe and the Near East. Bits of pocket lint could represent interest areas. We traveled by thumb, bus, train, ferryboat, motorcycle, and car for one year. Our aim was to participate in the lives of people who exist away from major routes of travel. We were constantly distracted into side trips, changing large plans to fit little events that became meaningful. Our general rule was to avoid recommendations, thus bypassing what were invariably tourist centers. If we were told not to go to some place because "it is nothing", "it" would often turn out to be fascinating. From our point of view, many coastlines have been ruined by tourism and trade. We had to give up looking for material along seacoasts, and learn to stay on inland routes.

The experience of travel in Turkey was a fantastic surprise in many dimensions—meeting with people, their hospitality, the changing landscape, and lush marketplaces. In Switzerland we seemed to meet our family, living high in the Alps. Possibly the highlight was a ten-week stay with a *Senn,* an alpine cheese maker; and an apprenticeship with a *Küfer-Meister*, the maker of milking buckets, butter churns, and other dairy implements used traditionally in the Alps.

Our visits to peasant farms were sources of inspiration and enlightenment concerning lifestyles that maximize the earth's productivity and conservation of natural resources. In Greece we saw tree trimmings brought to goats and sheep as fodder, and manure carted from animal stalls out to the orchards to fertilize soil. Walls of stone on terraced hillsides carefully cradle precious soil in Yugoslavia. We met a farmer in Switzerland who was harvesting trees planted by his father, and setting seedlings in the same woodlot so that his son can do the same. In Bulgaria we saw the materials and techniques of basketry applied to fences, roofing, corncribs, and buildings. We saw little waste. Many households and small communities exemplified an efficient and thorough use of their resources, as well as an understanding of natural limits.

By adopting local customs, we learned to appreciate our own resources. We found that the woolen and quilted clothing of some localities was sufficiently warm in unheated houses during moderately cold weather.

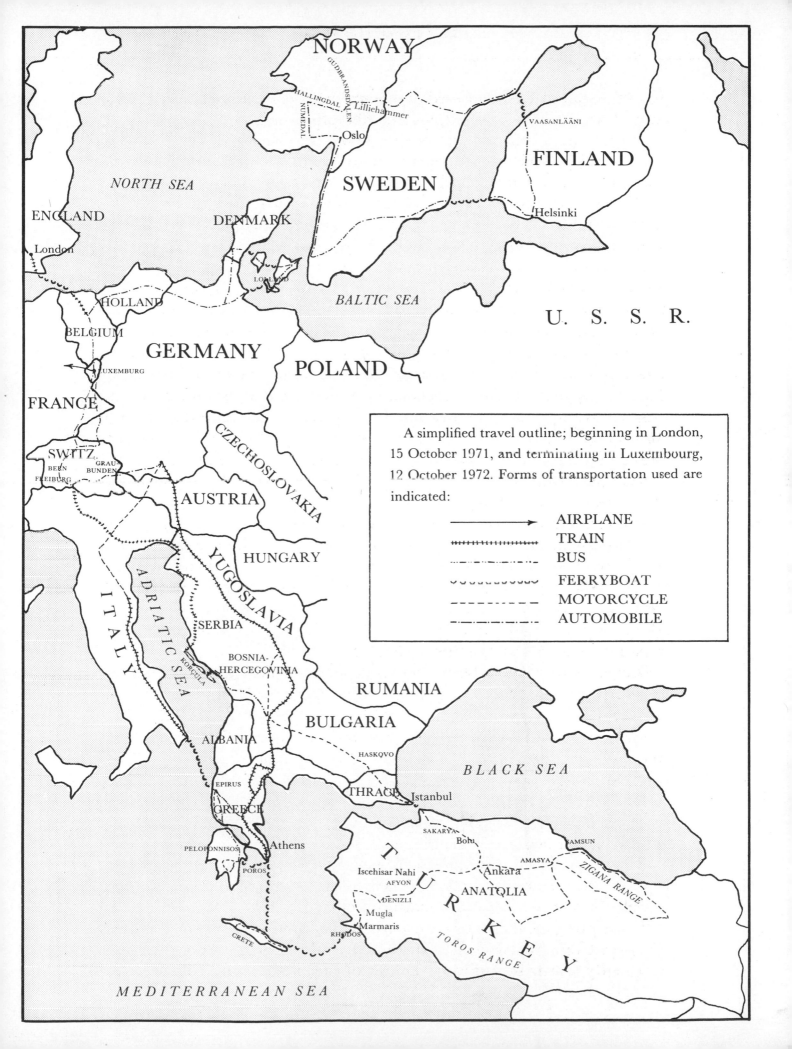

Washing clothes by hand at the village fountain can be entertaining as well as effective. Cutting timber with a bucksaw provides companionship and physical exercise as well as firewood. As Thoreau noted, ". . . it heats us twice; and the first warmth is the most wholesome and memorable, compared with the other is mere coke . . . the greatest value is received before the wood is teamed home."[2] We found this applicable to many tasks which allow us to use our bodies healthfully.

We particularly enjoyed helping harvest carefully nurtured produce of home gardens—often the only fertile spot in a sea of rock—or gathering wild plants for a delicious meal. We saw animals cared for with love, and began to understand the meaning of a feast involving the sacrifice of a lamb raised by the family. Houses built out of local materials with one's own time and energy created something personal and fitted to honest needs. We were often asked how we liked the purity and fragrance of the air, or quality of the spring water in a location. Our senses were especially aware in the silence of quiet days, hearing only a few chickens clucking about a courtyard.

The most successful farming ever done, in terms of sustained yield, soil maintenance and quality produce, has been done by hand and animal labor. In the United States, the Mennonites and Amish have consistently produced the finest crops, and received high returns for their efforts. In Switzerland a farmer may still plow behind draft horses and harvest with a hand scythe. One look at the members of his family or their fine hand-

Fig. 2–Cheese making in the Swiss Alps.

---

[2] Henry David Thoreau, *Journal*, November 22, 1853.

made farmhouse belies any statistic of poverty in the true sense. Perhaps most fantastic of all were the traditional farmers of the Far East. In China, a two and one-half acre farm could support a family of eleven, two cattle, one pig, and some chickens, besides bringing an income (just barely) adequate for buying provisions not raised or made at home.[3]

In this book we emphasize the importance of small, tenable cycles in the development of a better world community. In many instances handcrafts and hand farming may be found more efficient than mechanized techniques. Large scale agriculture is renowned for extremely high yields. However, statistics are complex. In terms of farmer's man-hours there is no argument. But the mechanized farmer is only an operator of one cog in a process that requires incredible amounts of fossil fuels, and draws on the combined energy of an entire economy.

"The replacement of the horse and the ox by the internal combustion engine and the electric motor is, however, attended by one great disadvantage. These machines do not void urine and dung, and so contribute nothing to the maintenance of soil fertility. No one has yet succeeded in establishing an efficient and permanent system of agriculture without livestock."[4] More precisely, ". . . for each unit of energy a Chinese wet rice farmer expends, he gets more than 50 in return; for each unit of fossil energy we expend, we get one-twentieth of a unit in return. On a basis of these ratios, Chinese wet rice agriculture is more than 1,000 times as efficient as our own system."

The energy deficit of "factory farming" results from the cost of producing chemical fertilizers, electricity, gasoline, and farm machinery—often using non-renewable resources.

It is through whole systems whose relationships with nature are understood that we choose to attempt our solutions. Simply put, a household which stocks whole grains and a handmill avoids rancid flour, loss of vitamins, and an exorbitant use of energy in processing and transportation. The satisfaction of feeling independent from the weight of a megalithic technology is another benefit of this practice. Foods taste better, bodies are healthier, even the frequency of dental caries is diminished. Other practices, such as raising one's food, composting wastes, building shelter from indigenous materials, and reforestation, involve more effort but yield greater returns for a healthy life and a sense of oneness and harmony. We are all living *off* the land, no matter where or how we do it. The possibility of living *with* the land is also open.

Drew AND Louise Langsner
Novato, California
October 29, 1973

---

[3] The thorough methods of these farmers, often working land under constant cultivation for thousands of years, are described by F. H. King in his classic work *Farmers of Forty Centuries*. Rodale Books, Inc. (reprint).

[4] Sir Albert Howard, *An Agricultural Testament.* Oxford University Press, 1943.

[5] According to Michael Perelman, University of California economist, in Jeff Cox's article "Factory Farming," *Organic Gardening and Farming*, June, 1973.

II. BALKAN ARCHITECTURE

THIS is a journey to rural villages and farmlands, down dirt roads and up mountainsides, into houses of stone, adobe or wood that are the homes of the people of the land. Most important, it is a journey into their lives—we want to know how they live, what grows in their fields and gardens, about their barns and kitchens.

The landscape is simple: rock, sun, and sea . . . land of vineyard and olives. A rough road winds through dry hills, connecting small villages. Stone houses cluster on hillsides like so many outcroppings of rock. Sometimes a red tile roof or a coat of whitewash punctuates the landscape.

3

4

FIGS. 3–6–Island of Korčula, Yugoslavia.

Along the Adriatic coastal mountains and throughout Greece, we found stone to be the most available and commonly used material. These lands, once rich and fertile, were long ago abused and stripped naked. Trees were cut for lumber and fuel (fossil fuels were unknown). Herding of sheep denuded the natural pasturage, leading to extensive erosion. Goats were left to range freely in the woods; their love for tender tree leaves hindered reforestation. The seas, once abundant with life, were fished beyond natural limits. Today the hilly land retains only scanty soil, collected into tiny terraced gardens, and found in cracks of mountain rock supporting minimal scrub and herbal growth. In coastal towns fishing has come almost to a standstill. The catch barely supports local needs.*

Traveling through these arid lands, we were continually impressed by the sheer quantity of rock. Fields everywhere are bordered by rock walls, often as wide as they are high. Old roadways were built of stone, sometimes laid two feet thick. Peasant houses, sheepherders' huts, animal shelters, bake ovens, storage sheds, well casings, cisterns, watering troughs, washtubs, and even kitchen sinks were stone.

---

* One island village that we visited (Vela Luka, Korčula, Yugoslavia) has a cannery, processing frozen fish from Japan. The small local fish market is sold out by 6 a.m.

The homes of these isolated rural folk are plain and unrefined. The feeling of rough rock predominates. In one house we noticed that the owner-builders had whitewashed the rocky hillside and attached three more stone walls to it. Little decorating or finishing is done beyond the coat of whitewash. The furnishing, sketched in Fig. 11, is crude and strictly utilitarian. One corner serves as a kitchen. This includes a table, or work counter, and a pantry nook set into the stone wall. Commonly seen is a commercially made tin storage closet with screen doors and sides, which is especially useful in summer for protecting food from flies. The sink is stone, often built into the ledge beneath a window. Water is stored in a ceramic urn, or in a tin reservoir hung just above the sink. Waste water drains out through a hole in the wall. Beds are wooden platforms. Mattresses consist of several thick, woven goat-hair rugs.

The architecture is seen in its most primitive form in Figs. 5 and 6—isolated field huts and old farmsteads. The plan is generally a narrow rectangle, usually one or two rooms, with a shed roof. Walls are 2' to 3' thick, and mortared with mud, if at all. The floor is earth or fieldstone. Ceilings are very low. Often these huts are dug into a hillside. This creates a sturdier structure, reduces drafts, and requires less detailed rock laying. The roof consists of a row of rafter poles, 2" to 4" in diameter, and spaced about one foot on center, supporting the flat roofing stones. If small, these are laid in courses, like tiles. Larger slabs—irregular pieces up to 20" by 30"—are placed in an overlapping pattern. In some districts, thatching is used (Chap. IX). Often there is no fireplace or smoke vent. There may be a stone hearth on the floor. Otherwise, a metal brazier is used. Regardless, smoke wafts about the room, eventually escaping through cracks in the ceiling. Woodwork is limited to door and casing work, and the board shutters which serve as windows. A row of sticks provides the simplest solution for spanning doorways and window openings. There is no toilet.

5

6

As the occupants live a primarily out-of-doors existence, these dwellings prove adequate for most occasions. Fresh air is appreciated and there are few possessions to lock up or keep indoors. Thick stone walls provide a cool shelter for hot summer days and for food storage. But in winter such a place is difficult to heat and often becomes damp from condensation. The solution is to wear many layers of woolen clothing.

A more elaborate construction is possible where lime mortar or portland cement and fired clay roofing tiles are available. Structures of a larger size are built, often two stories high (Fig. 8). The ground floor contains animal stalls and storage space (sometimes dug a few feet into the earth, like a semicellar). The upstairs serves as family living quarters. These larger buildings have less massive walls, 12″ to 15″ wide. Ceilings are not so low, and hip roof construction is most common (Fig. 10). This geometry is suitable, as it is well triangulated for strength. Rafter poles are short and may be quite thin. The use of tie beams is essential to keep the roof from spreading and forcing the walls apart. On the rafters is laid a course of bamboo poles or other lathing. Upon this is spread mortar to hold the roofing tiles in place. These are generally fired red clay, of the half-cylinder type called "Spanish tiles".

The upstairs plan includes several rooms connected by an interior hallway. One room is a combination bedroom and kitchen. This is the center for most indoor activities. Another is a formal dining or sitting room used on special occasions and furnished with family treasures—portraits of ancestors, wedding photographs, chests of formal clothing, a daughter's accumulating dowry of blankets, rugs, lace and embroidery made by her mother, and other keepsakes. The house may have one or two additional bedrooms.

Such a house has a fireplace located in the kitchen-bedroom. The style and construction peculiar to Greece seems to have evolved with two considerations: ease in construction and accessibility during cooking. At the rear of the fireplace the exterior dwelling wall does not extend outward. Rather, there is a shallow channel left open in the wall to form three sides of a chimney. Structurally, there is no integration of the fireplace and the house.

For cooking, this fireplace is very good. The hearth is accessible from three sides and is just the right height for someone working stooped close to the floor. There is plenty of room for moving pots around or for spreading out the fire. However it is a very poor heater (a blessing when cooking in hot weather). There is no smoke shelf or other provision for creating a draft; sometimes gusts of wind come down the chimney, blowing smoke and ashes about the room. When a fire is built forward, the room fills with smoke. If it is placed toward the rear, all the heat disappears up the huge smokehood. Fireplaces often have a cloth drape hanging from the mantel. This can be lowered to contain the smoke. Sometimes a chimney extension is added; a clay cylinder or length of stovepipe helps a great deal.

In these houses, windows are fitted with glass panes. The external shutters are often louvered. Flooring is generally pine, sometimes un-painted. The rest of the house is usually whitewashed, inside and out.

Fig. 7–Roofing of traditional tiles, and handmade chimney. Greece.

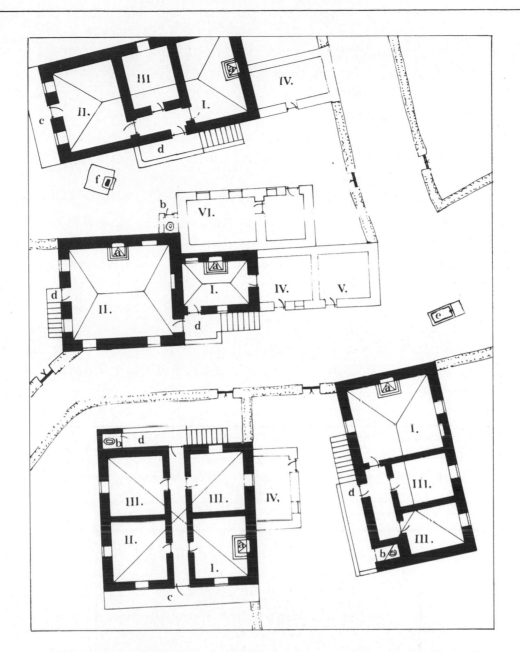

FIG. 8–Throughout the Balkans, farmers' houses are clustered into tiny villages. Each house has a small courtyard with perhaps a grape arbor, fruit trees, flowers, and a kitchen garden. This space is enclosed by stone walls and entered through gates. Many families live in two-story buildings. On the ground floor (shown in light outline) are generally storage sheds and animal stalls. These are shed-roof construction. Upstairs are the living quarters (shown in solid black). These larger dwellings have a hip or pyramid roof (indicated by thin lines crossing the floor plans). I. kitchen-bedroom; II. special dining room; III. bedroom; IV. shed; V. stall; VI. Grandparents' rooms (ground level). *a.* fireplace; *b.* privy; *c.* balcony; *d.* porch and staircase; *e.* fountain; *f.* bake oven.

The steps leading up to the main entrance are mortared stonework. Often an arch is formed underneath which leads to the ground floor storerooms. Generally a privy is attached to the upstairs porch, or to a shed in the yard. This facility is fitted with a ceramic toilet flushed by pouring a small bucket of water into the bowl. These houses have water piped into the kitchen. Electricity is now being installed, even in the outlying districts.

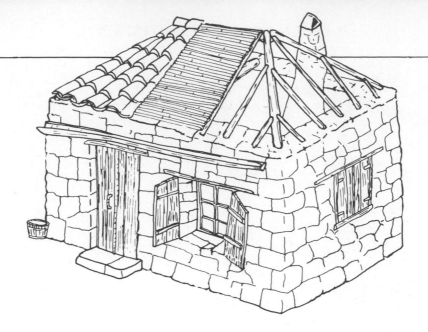

Fig. 9–Exposed roofing construction shows pole rafters, bamboo furring, and fired clay tiles. Woodwork includes carved rain gutter, lintels, board doors, shutters, and flooring. Glass is fitted in one window. Poros, Greece.

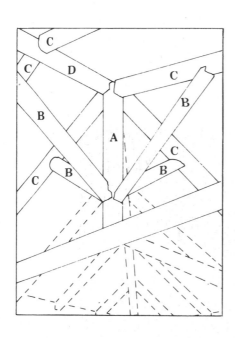

Fig. 10–Hip roof with furring strips that alternate sections of lumber and bamboo. A–B. kingpin truss; C. supporting rafters; D. ridgepole.

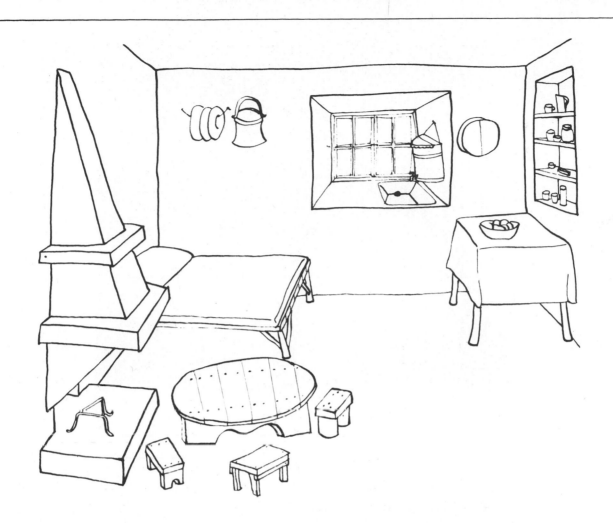

FIG. 11–The bedroom-kitchen of mountain goatherders. FIG. 12–
Roofing tiles and post and lintel construction details.

Fig. 13–Handmade terra-cotta roofing tiles hang on furring strips by a lip on the underside. Fig. 14–Ceramic tiles. Serbia, Yugoslavia.

III. GOAT HERDING

IN ancient times Greece was a rich and fertile land—truly a home of Gods, and suitable as the motherland of a civilization. But over the centuries, ravages of wars and invasions as well as faulty agricultural and herding practices have taken their toll on the land. Now the Hellenic peninsula is almost depleted of forest, soil and pasture resources.

The rocky, barren mountains of Greece are the domain of great numbers of goats.* These animals are browsers, prefering to eat from shrubs and trees. Sheep are grass grazers and must be pastured down beneath the olive trees and on other marginal land. Unlike cows, both sheep and goats can survive on very scanty vegetation. They consume little water, and tolerate a saline content almost twice that of cattle.

Herds continue to devour whatever greenery is left as they roam the countryside; but they are providers of livelihood. From goats and sheep come milk for rich yogurt and cheeses, and meat for the traditional Easter Feast. Skins, wool, hair, and manure are also valuable.

FIG. 15–Mountain goats. Greece.

* Socialism in Yugoslavia has brought about national programs to protect and develop natural resources. The need for reforestation was seen; and keeping goats made illegal. For village farmers this presented a limited hardship. But the hill people, dependent on their herds, and living on the worst land, were left helpless. Most gave up their traditional existence. But some are left, living hidden in the back country and thin forests with outlaw herds.

Sheep and goats are herded daily throughout the year from pasture to pasture. Sheep, if confined to a small area, mow their pasturage down to root level. Goats can denude everything within reach, and being able climbers, even mount trees to reach the freshest leaflets. The dry mountainsides have been their range for so long that they must climb about the rocky gorges constantly in order to scavenge enough food.

Evidence of herds and flocks is ubiquitous in the Greek countryside. The ringing of countless distant bells sounds from the hillsides; the wilderness is threaded with goat trails and strewn with droppings. But existence of the herder is more ephemeral.

Often we saw men and women tending their flocks on hillside olive groves, or moving slowly down the road amid a cloud of dust and fleece. Sometimes they passed through our village, directing herds with shouts in their peculiar herders' language: *Hey!*

Hey, hey, hey, hey, hey,
Ya – hey!
Waiiii. . . . .
Tsuh! Tsuh! Tsuh!
ppppppppptsai!

These men and women are relics of the past—with shepherd's crooks and black, homespun woolen clothing. Trekking over the hills with their animals from morning until evening (in all weather) and living in isolated settlements, the herders are not integrated into village life and have not entered into modern times.

FIG. 16–Goatherders' settlement. Greece.

Fig. 17– Georgios and Dimitra milking mountain goats from between the hind legs. Average yield in March is less than 1 cup per animal. The daughter keeps the goats moving forward in the funnel-shaped enclosure.

One day we set out for the mountains to wander about on the goat trails. Our hike took us up a dirt road that ended at a water fountain and a cluster of dwellings (Fig. 16). A rocky trail continued further, leading us into the midst of some fifty kid goats feasting on a pile of olive trimmings. Here we met Georgios, the herder. He came from his work in the nearby goat shelter and called for us to stop and visit. We sat together on the rock wall of a corral while he rolled a cigarette, explaining that he grew the tobacco. Soon a young girl appeared, bringing glasses of cold water and a plate of salty olives and *feta* cheese. When he could not convince us to take any more refreshment, and we had answered as many questions about ourselves as a limited knowledge of Greek would allow, he led us up the mountainside to see his small fields of grain, tobacco and olive trees. Georgios didn't walk, but jogged over the rocks with a loose rhythm that suggested an ability to continue for hours.

Later, we went to the house—two rooms of whitewashed stone built partially into the hillside. The front room was formally set to receive visitors; the second room is where most of the household activity takes place. This is the room shown in Fig. 11. As the sun was setting a faint tinkling of bells announced the return of Georgios' wife, Dimitra, from her day of herding on the mountain. She soon appeared at the door—eyes shining and face rosy from her trek—to welcome us, serve coffee, and then insist that we extend our visit overnight.

After accepting, we went out to watch evening milking. The daughter, Evangelia, was waiting on the rocks with the herd, which she drove with shouts, whistles, and armwaving into a funnel-shaped brush enclosure. In Fig. 17 Georgios and Dimitra are sitting on two rocks at the narrow end of the enclosure. Evangelia kept the goats moving forward. As each goat passed through the opening she was stopped and milked from between her hind legs. In about one hour, nearly one hundred goats were milked.

The total milking was less than five gallons. As well as being small, these mountain goats must expend a great deal of energy each day; their yield is very low. Such poor land could not support larger animals. This is why it is necessary for each herding family to maintain many animals, including bucks and kids.

When they were finished the milk was emptied through a clean cloth filter into another bucket and hung from the limb of a tree. The pails were washed with hot water. It was dark when we returned to the house for supper.

The meal was simple. Evangelia built a fire, and Dimitra made a thick soup of *hilopites* (page 37). Georgios took a doughnut-shaped bread from a string of loaves hanging on the wall and cut thick slices. A low table was brought forward, and we pulled stools close around the fireplace. Soon after dinner we were ready to sleep.

FIG. 18–Kid enclosure.

FIG. 19–Wheelbarrow. Yugoslavia.

It was still dark when we heard Georgios going out the door. We asked if it was time for milking. "No, it is still night. We will milk in the morning." We looked at our watch. It was four o'clock. Later, we learned Georgios had gone out to round up the goats, which are allowed to wander freely during the night.

As the sun rose we could hear Dimitra and Evangelia building a fire and sweeping the other room. We got up and made a cup of mountain herb tea before going with them to the pens. There we found work: washing milk cans, feeding the kids, and sweeping up with stiff brush brooms. In about an hour, Georgios appeared with the goats and milking got underway. Afterwards, all the milk, including the last night's, was poured into two flat-sided cans and tied onto a donkey to be taken down the road for truck pickup (Fig. 21).

By the time milking was over, the herd had begun to nibble its way up the mountain. Dimitra followed along the trail, whistling and calling out directions. She moved quickly over the well-grazed route to the back side of the hill and paused to let the goats browse. They trimmed the scant vegetation, then moved ahead. We climbed all morning in the warm sun, stopping often for the goats.

By midday we reached the top of a ridge, where we stopped for a lunch of bread, cheese, and olives. We rested, watching tiny figures of men and mules cultivating fields far below. We could see flocks of sheep moving beneath olive trees and heavily loaded donkeys on the dusty road. Hills stretched out in the distance, small villages were tucked here and there, and the ocean filled out the horizon.

Afternoon passed as the morning: moving with the herd over the rocks, standing or sitting in the sun, continually moving. As the sun sank in the sky, we turned around and began our homeward journey. We didn't stop, but moved steadily amid a jostling sea of ringing bells. Darkness was approaching by the time we reached the milking area.

CHEESE MAKING

Cheese making is based on simple principles modified in different ways to produce the wonderful cheeses that we like to eat. The cheese maker is concerned with curd, whey, fat content, and age of milk. Curd is that part of milk which will coagulate or solidify. Whey is the watery element which remains.

For the simplest cheeses (soft and fresh), curd and whey are separated by letting raw milk stand overnight in a warm place. The curd is then tied into a cloth and hung to drain until thickened. A little salt is added and this cheese is ready to be eaten.

Other cheeses are curdled by dispersing an activating agent called rennet into milk that has been warmed.

Cheese making uses large quantities of milk. The weight of a finished cheese is approximately one-tenth of the original milk. The remaining whey can be used as a beverage—fresh, soured, or fermented. It is excellent in breads, soups, grain, and other dishes. Whey is high in lactose, and may be boiled down to a readily digestible sugar. Whey may also be fed to chickens and hogs; however, large quantities will cause diarrhea when given to other animals. Another use for whey is as a washing and bleaching agent. Wooden utensils washed in whey develop a waxy finish. Washing oneself in warm whey is good for the skin.

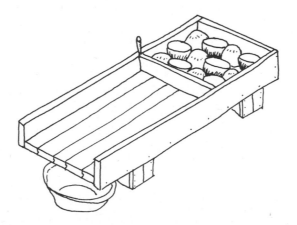

FIG. 20–Curing *feta* cheese. Our neighbor, a woman named Marina, bought already-formed cheeses from a shepherd's wife. Every other morning, for about two weeks, the lady delivered 2 cheeses which she carried hung from a stick balanced across her shoulders. After the cheeses were weighed and paid for, they were set onto a special curing table—a large wooden box 30 inches wide, and 8 feet long, with one end-board missing. Several days before curing began, the table surface was flooded with a milk-like water and flour solution to swell the joints. The apparatus was then placed in the basement on crates at a slight angle. A large wash pan was set beneath the lower, open end.

FETA CHEESE

Feta, the most common cheese in Greece, is eaten plain, with olives or salads, and is used in baking. *Feta* is white, rather soft, crumbly and salty. To make *feta* cheese, fresh goat's or sheep's milk is used. Rennet is made from the stomach of a kid or lamb not yet weaned (having had a diet of mostly milk) or one that is less than 40 days old.

Preparing rennet: Take the stomach, tie off one end, and fill with fresh milk. Then tie the other end. Hang in the sun to dry until contents become cheesy, and the skin is parched.

Making feta: Very slowly heat a large quantity of fresh milk (at least 10 quarts) to a temperature described as "pretty hot, but o.k. to touch." Cut off a piece of rennet (approximately one-fifth stomach per 10 quarts milk) and tie in a cloth sack. Immerse sack in the warm milk. When rennet softens, squeeze the contents out of the sack, dispersing it throughout the milk. Stir continually for 1 hour, until milk curdles. With hands, squish curd around. Carefully transfer curd into a cheesecloth and tie the four corners together. Hang to drain overnight.

Curing: First sprinkle crude sea salt where the *feta* will lie. Then cut cheese in half (each round ball weighs 5 to 6 lbs.). Lay cheeses on the salted surface. Rub salt lightly on the tops. Shove cheeses firmly against the back board. Push another board against cheeses, and wedge tightly in place. Every 8 hours *feta* must be turned and resalted. Continue for 7 to 10 days, depending on size of the cheese and saltiness desired. (A smaller cheese requires much less salt and curing time.) Salt draws moisture out of the *feta*, and the resulting brine drips into the pan. Freshly made *feta* is very soft, rather squishy, and sweet tasting. Each day the cheese is firmer and drier. When ready, it is salty and slightly crumbly. Cured *feta* is stored in its own salt brine, usually in a ceramic crock kept in a cool place.

Although goat's or sheep's milk and natural rennet are not generally available, it is possible to make *feta* using substitute ingredients. Cow's milk (preferably raw) and commercial rennet preparations* may be used.

Variation: In a small bowl dissolve commercial rennet (1 tablet per gallon milk) into ⅓ cup lukewarm water. Stir mixture into prewarmed milk; let stand for 15 or 20 minutes, until a curd forms. This is like custard. Continue making *feta* using the given instructions.

---

* Two brands of rennet are: Hansen's Cheese Rennet Tablets (Chr. Hansen Laboratory, Inc.; 9015 W. Maple St; Milwaukee, Wis.), and Junket Tablets, found in some markets and drug stores.

IV. BALKAN COOKING

THE ADRIATIC COAST AND HELLENIC PENINSULA

IN the ancient countryside of the Adriatic coast and Hellenic peninsula, people live much as their ancestors did hundreds of years ago. The landscape is that of ageless sun, rock, and sea. Dusty roads thread into the hills, past stone-walled terraces and grey-green olive trees, to villages of red tile roofs and whitewashed stone. Houses sit behind walled and vine-shaded yards, clustered on the hillside with a Byzantine church in their midst.

Farming is the main occupation, grapes and olives the major crops. Wheat, cabbages, beans, tomatoes, tobacco and cotton grow in small plots. Figs and almonds are common, and cherries, apricots, and walnuts occasionally found; oranges and lemons are found in pockets of alluvial flatland along the coast. In addition to a trellis of table grapes, most homes include a small, but abundant, vegetable plot. Chickens generally live in a hut behind the house and wander freely about the yard.

Donkeys and mules provide personal transportation and power for plowing. Villagers leave their houses early in the morning, leading or riding their animals to fields in the surrounding hills. Cultivation of the extremely rocky soil within narrow, and often steep, terraces does not lend itself to mechanization; pruning of vines and trees, as well as harvesting crops, are tasks suited to hand farming techniques. When the farmers return to their village at dusk, the donkeys are heavily laden with tree prunings for use as fodder and fuel.

FIG. 21–Packing sheep's milk to the highway for truck pickup.
FIG. 22– Picking olives. Yugoslavia.

Fig. 23.

Much of the rocky land is unsuitable for any farming and is grazed by herds of goats and sheep. One or two of these animals are also part of almost every village household, as they are kept for wool and milk. These beautiful, long-haired goats and sheep are tended lovingly; each day the owners lead them to the orchards to graze beneath trees; or bundles of olive prunings are brought home as food. Village animals are of larger breeds than the mountain herds and give more milk, which is made into yogurt or cheese. Male lambs or kids are raised to the age of a few months, when they are slaughtered and spitted to serve the occasion of a family celebration or a holiday feast.

Although the soil is long spent of its original fertility, and the harvest is simple, food and wine are among the great delights of the people who inhabit this land. The long summer sun ripens fruits and vegetables to perfection, and there is a fine yield of rich milk for making cheese and yogurt. Other specialties include home-pressed olive oil, homemade wine, golden crusted breads, and fresh seafood. Even a herder's meal of salt-cured olives and *feta* cheese seems a delicious feast. Luckily, the farm families are always ready to stop work in the cause of hospitality. Refreshment is certain to be offered, and the spirit of enjoyment is shared as generously with the visitor as the food itself.

KAFFA, KAFE, or *KAHVE* Turkish Coffee

An invitation to coffee is a special welcome and an introduction to Balkan hospitality—the warming experience of an opening door and sharing of food and company. Coffee served in both Yugoslavia and Greece is really Turkish style, brought to the Balkan countries with the spread of the Ottoman Empire (which at its peak extended east to the Arabian Sea, north to the Black Sea, south to include Egypt and most of North Africa, and west throughout the entire Balkan peninsula). This is a very simple coffee, strong and black, and usually served with some kind of sweet and a glass of cold spring water. The "best ever" we tasted was made by a Yugoslav lady, carefully brewed and set on the table with *lumblije* (spice bread) and *orahovica* (homemade walnut brandy). The coffee is made from strong, dark-roasted beans, freshly ground into fine powder. Turkish coffeepots* work best. Copper or enameled, they come in sizes measured exactly for one to several servings (2 to 3 ounces per person).

For two servings, measure 4 to 6 oz. water into the pot. Heat to boiling. Remove from fire and pour off about 1½ tsp. hot water into a cup. Add 2 tsp. sugar and 3 heaping tsp. coffee to water in pot. Stir well to dissolve. Replace pot on low fire. Heat slowly until foam rises. Remove from heat and quickly pour reserve water over foam. Stir once. Pour coffee into cups in small amounts, alternating to distribute foam and grounds equally. Allow coffee to sit a few moments before drinking.

Quality and patience are key ingredients. Beans should be freshly ground (even fresh-roasted, if possible); this is when the coffee is at its peak in aroma and flavor. Also, brew it slowly. The best method is to set the pot into the dying embers of a fire, allowing it to heat 5 to 10 minutes; extra time to enjoy the aroma and a truly delicious coffee are the results.

---

* In Greece, *briki*; in Turkey, *ibriği*.

HOMEMADE SPIRITS

Orahovica is a Yugoslav walnut brandy. To make this, you will need 5 or 6 walnuts inside their green husks (these must be picked off a tree), 1 quart white brandy, and ½ lb. sugar. With a sharp fork make several pokes through the husks to each nut. Place in a ceramic crock and cover with sugar and brandy. Cover with a gauze cloth, and set in the sunshine for one month. Strain and bottle.

Mediterranean *Tangerine Brandy* is bottled sunshine for a stormy winter evening. You must have 20 to 30 "*extra prima*" tangerines, ½ lb. sugar, and 1 quart brandy. Peel and section tangerines. Break peels into small pieces and place with sections in a ceramic crock. Cover with sugar and brandy. Cover the crock with gauze cloth; let sit in the sun for 40 days. Strain and bottle.

Cherry Liqueur. Ingredients: 2 lbs. sweet, ripe cherries, 2 quarts brandy, ½ lb. sugar, 3 sticks cinnamon, 30 cloves. Pit cherries. Place all ingredients in a crock. Cover with a gauze cloth and set in the sun for 40 days. Strain and bottle.

HORTA

While pasturing sheep or goats, the women are often busy gathering herbs for their family table. Throughout the year an abundance of wild edible greens can be gathered. These are used as potherbs and are called *horta*. The name looks like this: *XOPTA,* in Greek. The women are familiar with a wide variety of plants, and with the locations most favorable for finding choice specimens. For instance, a fallow field after winter rains have begun is an excellent place to find baskets of delicious young *manganithes* (poppy greens). In all cases, young shoots, flower buds, and the tender center growth of older plants are gathered. For the following recipes, use available fresh greens. Suitable domestic greens include mustard, dandelion, rapini, escarole, endive, spinach, turnip, and beet. Combining different varieties makes the flavor more interesting.

HORTA VRASTA   Boiled Greens

2 to 3 lbs. mixed greens   **olive oil**
salt   **lemon juice**

Wash greens carefully, drain, and steam or parboil until tender. Place in a bowl and serve with olive oil, lemon juice, salt and pepper. Delicious hot or cold.

POTATOES AND HORTA

4 to 6 potatoes   **¼ cup olive oil**
2 lbs. mixed greens   **juice of 1 lemon**
salt and pepper

Boil potatoes until tender, but not mushy. Cook greens separately. Dice cooked potatoes and place in a bowl. Sprinkle with salt, pepper, oil and lemon juice. Drain and chop cooked greens; combine with potatoes. Serve hot.

HORTA WITH TOMATO SAUCE

¼ cup olive oil   **1 Tbs. fresh mint**
1 onion, chopped   **2 bay leaves**
2 cloves garlic, pressed **2 lbs. mixed greens**
½ cup chopped parsley   **salt**
6 to 8 fresh tomatoes   **fresh lemon**
1 Tbs. oregano

Heat 2 Tbs. oil in a large skillet; sauté onion, garlic, and parsley for 5 minutes. Add sliced tomatoes and stir to heat thoroughly. Add oregano, mint, bay leaves, and remaining oil. Simmer 15 to 20 minutes. Wash, drain, and cook greens. Place greens in a serving bowl. Pour tomato sauce on top. Serve hot with salt and pepper. A squeeze of fresh lemon makes this extra special.

SOUPA

The warm, fragrant kitchen of a good Greek cook is an excellent place to seek refuge on cold, rainy days. This is how we gleaned our knowledge of Greek cooking and many wonderful meals. One friend's kitchen was particularly well arranged for open-fire cooking. A large fireplace was set into the wall at a height of 30 inches, with a ledge extending out in front. An iron tripod was set over the fire to hold a cookpot, and a separate tray for holding hot coals was used with a grill for toasting bread or chestnuts. Shiny copper pots of all sizes sat on a shelf above the fireplace, while a cupboard below the work ledge held bottles of oil, a keg of salt, and a good supply of wood.

FASSOLADA　Bean Soup

This is Greek soup, the first course of a very Greek meal of tiny fried fishes, salty olives, *feta* cheese and *retsina*.

1 to 2 cups white beans	4 to 6 cups beef broth or vegetable stock
olive oil	1 tsp. salt
1 large onion	4 pepper corns
2 cloves garlic	2 bay leaves
1 or 2 carrots	1 tsp. oregano
1 cup chopped celery	4 Tbs. chopped parsley
1 cup diced potato	fresh lemons
6 to 8 fresh tomatoes	

Soak beans overnight in water to cover. Rinse well and drain. Heat olive oil in a large soup kettle. Sauté chopped onion, garlic, carrots, celery, potato, and tomatoes until onion is transparent. Add beans, broth, salt, pepper, and bay leaves; mix well. Bring to a boil; then simmer (covered) over low fire 45 minutes. Add water, if necessary, to keep beans covered. Add oregano and parsley; simmer 15 to 20 minutes longer, or until beans are tender. Serve with slices of lemon, freshly ground black pepper, and a good crusty bread. This is a hearty, homey soup; the squeeze of fresh lemon lets the spirit soar.

SOUPA AVGHO-LEMONO   Egg-Lemon Soup

½ chicken (or 1 lb. meat or fish)	2 eggs, separated
5 cups water	juice of 1 lemon
1 cup rice (or *manestra**)	parsley
1 tsp. salt	black pepper

Cut chicken into serving pieces and put it with water and salt into a large pot over the fire. Bring to a boil for a few minutes, then skim foam from the surface. Simmer gently until meat is tender, about one half-hour. Remove pieces from the pot and strain broth. (Wash out pot.) Return meat and broth to the pot and bring to boil again. Add rice; simmer, stirring occasionally, until cooked. When soup is ready, beat egg whites with 1 Tbs. cold water in a shallow bowl until thick and frothy. Then beat egg yolks and lemon juice into the whites. Remove soup from fire and spoon 6 Tbs. broth into the egg-lemon mixture, stirring constantly with a fork. Pour entire mixture into the soup. Stir gently over heat, but do not allow to boil. Garnish with sprigs of parsley. Serve at once, and pass the pepper grinder.

Variations: 1. Omit chicken; use broth or vegetable stock only. 2. Make soup with chopped celery hearts. 3. Add one cup cream or sour cream to broth before stirring in egg-lemon mixture.

---

* *Manestra* is a grain-sized Greek pasta.

AVGHO-LEMONO SALTSA   Egg-Lemon Sauce

2 to 4 eggs, separated
juice of 2 lemons
1 cup broth or stock, boiling hot

Beat egg whites until stiff. Add egg yolks and continue beating. Slowly pour in lemon juice, beating constantly. Beat in hot stock, 1 Tbs. at a time. This sauce is poured over vegetables, stuffed cabbage or vine leaves, fish, stew, and soups. If the dish was cooked in liquid, this stock should be used for the sauce.

SOUPA TRACHANA

2 to 3 Tbs. olive oil	1 bay leaf
1 onion	1 cup *trachana**
2 cups stewed tomatoes	1 to 2 cups egg-lemon sauce (optional)
2 celery stalks with leaves	salt and pepper
2 cups chicken broth	

Heat olive oil in the bottom of a heavy soup kettle. Sauté chopped onion until transparent before adding tomatoes, chopped celery, chicken broth, and bay leaf. Bring to a boil, cover, and simmer 15 to 20 minutes. Strain and reserve the broth. Bring broth to a boil, and stir in *trachana*. Simmer until thick (about 25 minutes). Make egg-lemon sauce with additional chicken broth, and stir into soup, following directions given in *Soupa Avgho-Lemono* recipe.

---

* *Trachana* is cracked wheat pasta made in Greece (refer to pg. 37).

PITA

Pita is a fantastic creation akin to pie. Various fillings may be found between many layers of paper-thin sheets of pastry called *filo*. *Filo* can be purchased at Greek or Turkish specialty stores; it can also be made at home. The latter requires practice and patience to roll the dough to the proper thinness. We watched a Greek woman using a broom-handle-like rolling stick to roll circles of dough 2 feet in diameter and almost transparent. She was an expert, and her dough was no more than flour, salt, oil, and hot water. For the beginner, a yeasted dough and smaller sized *pita* are advisable.

FILO

1 cup milk	1 Tbs. dry active yeast, dissolved
1 cup butter	in ¼ cup lukewarm water
2 lbs. pastry flour	1 tsp. salt

Scald milk. Melt butter in hot milk. When mixture is cooled to lukewarm, add yeast dissolved in water. Sprinkle on salt; then gradually mix in flour to make a smooth dough. Knead dough 10 minutes on a floured surface. Cover with a damp cloth and let rise until double in size. Allow a large, smooth space for rolling out *filo*. Punch down dough and cut into 8 sections (a *pita* requires 4 bottom and 4 top sheets of hand-rolled pastry). Roll 1 section into a smooth ball; cover remaining dough with a damp cloth. Press the ball into a flat circle ½ inch thick. Use a 1 inch dowel about 30 inches long as a rolling stick. Begin to roll the flattened ball with the stick, keeping dough circular. When the *filo* is 10 to 12 inches in diameter, flour lightly and roll up evenly onto the stick. Roll *filo* over itself, kneading down gently and evenly. Unroll, flour, and roll up again (changing the edges). Repeat until *filo* is as thin as possible. Roll out 8 layers of *filo*. Use a round, 3-inch deep baking pan, or cut the *filo* to fit a square pan. Bottom layers should be slightly larger than the pan so that edges fold in to hold the filling which should be ready when the *filo* is being made.

INDIVIDUAL *PITES*

Instead of one *pita* made with large sheets of *filo*, many small *pites* can be made like turnovers. If using homemade *filo*, pinch off enough dough for one small *pita*, a circle 4 to 6 inches across. Roll out each lump of dough as thinly as possible to this diameter. Place a spoonful of any filling in the center, then fold in half. Press edges to seal. Place *pites* on cookie sheets; brush each with butter, and bake at 375° for 10 to 15 minutes.

If using store bought *filo*, cut the sheets into long strips, 3 inches wide, and brush with melted butter. Place 1 tsp. filling at the bottom of each strip and fold one corner up to form a triangle; continue folding in a triangular shape until the entire strip is folded. Bake as above, or fry in hot olive oil. Serve hot.

TIROPITA   Cheese Pita

Tiropita is a cheese-filled pastry sold in every *kafenion* (café), and from pushcarts in the streets. The cheese is salty *feta*, white and crumbly.

1 lb. store bought *filo*, **or 8 layers hand-rolled** *filo*	**3 eggs, separated**
1 lb. *feta* **cheese**	**¾ to 1 cup olive oil, or melted butter**
½ cup heavy cream	**freshly ground black pepper**

Beat egg yolks with cream and 1 tsp. oil. Crumble *feta* into tiny pieces and mix into liquid. Grind in a generous amount of pepper. Fold in stiffly beaten egg whites. Roll out *filo*, as described on preceding page, or stack ready-made *filo* on a table or counter top. (Note: *filo* dries out quickly and must be covered with a damp towel.) Grease a large baking pan (about 15 inches diameter, or 12 x 15 inches rectangular). Put oil or butter in a small bowl. Brush the first pastry sheet with oil, and fit it into the pan, allowing edges to hang over the sides. Continue with 4 sheets handmade, or half of total ready-made *filo*. Turn each sheet slightly, rather than placing it squarely on top of the others. This will make a fanned-out edge. Pour in filling and spread evenly. Fold over pastry edges to hold filling, brushing again with oil or butter. If pastry sheets are very large, they may cover *pita* entirely, in which case only 3 or 4 more sheets will be needed to make the top crust. Otherwise, brush remaining sheets with oil and place them on top, trimming down to the size of pan. Brush 2 or 3 Tbs. oil or butter over the top. With a sharp knife cut through *pita* in parallel, then diagonal, rows to make diamonds. Bake at 350° for 30 to 45 minutes, or until golden brown. Serve hot.

SPANAKOPITA   Spinach *Pita*

A most enjoyable *pita*, and a delicious way to eat spinach.

½ lb. store bought *filo*, **or 8 sheets hand-rolled** *filo*	**freshly ground black pepper**
3 lbs. fresh spinach	**1 lb.** *feta* **cheese**
1 handful fresh dill	**3 to 6 eggs**
1 bunch scallions	**1½ cups olive oil**

Wash spinach well and cut off stems. Chop or tear leaves into tiny pieces. Chop scallions and dill, and add to spinach in a large bowl. Pour on ½ cup olive oil, rubbing with hands until leaves are well coated. Mix in crumbled *feta* and pepper. Stir in beaten eggs. *Spanakopita* may be prepared with top and bottom layers of *filo*, as in *tiropita*. Or it can be made in a long roll. To do this, lay out 3 or 4 sheets *filo* on top of each other, brushing each with oil. (If using store bought *filo,* prepare half of the total amount for each roll. Place sheets carefully, one on top of the other, brushing each with olive oil.) Spoon the spinach filling out along one edge, and turn filo over to make a roll. Brush with oil while rolling the *filo*. Seal the edge and place in a greased baking pan. Slash through *filo* in 2 inch sections. Make 2 rolls. Bake at 375° for one-half hour. This is best eaten hot, fresh from the oven.

HORTOPITA

Pita with a filling of *horta* (wild greens) is particularly pungent. This is how we discovered the delights of eating poppies. A mixture of garden greens is also good, especially if some of the spicier ones are included. Then it is called *lachanopita*.

1 lb. store bought *filo*, or
    6 to 8 layers hand-rolled pastry
2 to 3 lbs. greens
1 bunch scallions

1 handful fresh dill
olive oil
salt and pepper
½ cup minced parsley

Preparation is similar to *spanakopita*. Use available fresh greens such as spinach, mustard, dandelion, etc. Rub washed and chopped greens well with olive oil to reduce volume. Add pepper, salt and herbs. Spread greens between top and bottom layers of *filo* (each sheet brushed with oil) in a large baking pan. Brush 2 to 3 Tbs. oil over top *filo*. Cut into pieces. Bake at 350° for 30 to 45 minutes. Serve hot.

TZADZIKI AND THICK YOGURT

Tzadziki is a powerful Greek specialty used as a dip or spread for bread. Good with *retsina*.

1 cup thick yogurt
large clove garlic, pressed

2 Tbs. minced onion
salt

Yogurt is thickened by hanging in a muslin cloth overnight, allowing it to drain. The result is a kind of tart cream cheese. Mix garlic, onion, and salt into the thick yogurt. Let stand 1 hour to mingle flavors before serving.

MOUSAKÁS

Mousakás is a layered casserole of eggplant and ground meat, covered with white sauce. There are many variations, depending on the cook and the vegetables in season.

2 or 3 eggplants
salt and pepper
2 onions, chopped
2 cloves garlic, chopped
2 lbs. ground lamb
¼ tsp. cinnamon
¼ tsp. nutmeg

½ tsp. oregano
½ cup parsley leaves
1 Tbs. fresh mint
1 cup tomato sauce
olive oil
2 to 4 cups white sauce
grated cheese

Slice eggplants ½ inch thick. Sprinkle slices with salt and set aside on a clean towel. Heat oil in a large skillet. Sauté onion and garlic briefly; then add meat, seasoned with salt and freshly ground black pepper. Crumble meat with a fork, and stir until evenly browned. Add spices, herbs, and tomato suace. Mix well, and simmer 15 to 20 minutes. Wipe the salted eggplant. Sauté slices quickly over high heat in a small amount of oil. Set aside to drain.

Prepare the white sauce as follows: in top of a double boiler, heat 4 Tbs. butter until bubbly. Carefully stir in 4 Tbs. flour, and cook a few minutes. Slowly add 2 cups hot milk, stirring constantly with a wire whisk. Let the sauce thicken. Season with salt and pepper. Remove from heat, cool, and add 3 beaten egg yolks.

Assemble *mousakás* in a large greased casserole. Arrange a layer of eggplant on the bottom, spread the meat mixture over this and sprinkle on grated cheese. Make another layer of eggplant, more grated cheese, and cover with white sauce. Top generously with grated cheese. Add another layer of eggplant, more grated cheese, and cover with white sauce. Top generously with grated cheese. Bake at 350° for 1 hour.

Variations: Substitute for the eggplant 2 lbs. zucchini or 2 lbs. potatoes; cut in ¼ inch slices and sauté. One may also include (or substitute) a layer of macaroni, cooked and mixed with melted butter and beaten eggs.

FISH and MEAT

The preparation of fish and meat throughout the Balkan countries is often done over a bed of hot coals on a grill or rotating spit. Many homes still have the traditional cookhouse, a small outbuilding with an open hearth where a grill may be placed (smoke escapes through spaces between the roof tiles).

MARINADE SAUCE

2 cups wine	1 Tbs. thyme
1 cup olive oil	2 bay leaves
1 Tbs. oregano	½ cup chopped parsley
1 Tbs. rosemary	juice of 3 lemons

Combine ingredients. Use red wine for meat and white wine for fish and poultry. Marinate the fish or meat overnight, then baste with the marinade during cooking.

PSARI PLAKI   Fish Bake

This is baked in a heavy iron pot with tightly fitting lid, set on a tripod over hot coals on the open hearth.

1 to 2 lbs. baking fish	3 fresh tomatoes, sliced
1 cup parsley leaves	2 cloves garlic, pressed
1 bunch scallions	½ cup olive oil
juice of 1 lemon	1 cup water, or wine
salt and pepper	oregano
2 large onions, thinly sliced	lemon slices
1 bell pepper, sliced	

Scale, clean and wash fish. Spread ½ cup parsley and chopped scallions in the bottom of a greased casserole. Arrange fish on top and squeeze on lemon juice. Sprinkle with salt and grind on pepper. Combine onions, pepper, tomatoes, garlic, oregano, and remaining parsley with olive oil and wine; mix and pour over fish. Place lemon slices on top of fish; bake at 350° for 1 hour, basting occasionally. Serve with fresh tomato slices, a crusty bread, and *retsina*.

SKEMBE   Kid Goat Intestines

This recipe was prepared by our goat-herding friends, and served with fresh bread, salty olives, and *retsina* (all homemade).

Intestines from one kid may be 50 to 60 feet long. Cut these into 2 foot strips, and wash thoroughly in cold water. Loop 6 lengths around a convenient knob, making 12 strands. Divide into thirds and braid, tying off at the end with the longest piece. Repeat with the remaining strips. Put braided intestines into a frying pan and half cover with water. Simmer half-hour, turning pieces every 5 minutes while skimming the water clean. When tender, drain water and add ⅔ cup olive oil. Cover with a lid and braise 10 minutes, turning pieces often. When slightly crisp, remove from fire and add salt, freshly ground black pepper, and a liberal amount of lemon juice.

SARACOSTI

Saracosti is a time of purification observed by the Greek Orthodox Church, known as Lent in Western countries. Beginning 50 days before Easter Sunday, the Orthodox congregation fasts from animal foods—cheese, milk, butter, eggs, meat, fish, and poultry. More popular than the weeks of fasting is the day of feasting preceding *Saracosti*. For this, elaborate meals are prepared with roast turkey or chicken, with rich custards of milk and eggs for dessert.

The first day of *Saracosti* is a feast in its own right. The special fast foods are fish roe or sea urchin roe, octopus, squid, mussels (we were told "these don't have blood"), olives, halvah, and *dolmathes*—rice-stuffed vine leaves (see *dolma*, Chap. VI). A sesame-coated flat bread called *lagana* is eaten with these delicacies. Almost everyone partakes of the fast this day, and there is much visiting and sharing of foods.

COLIVA

Coliva is made by the women of each household on the eve of *Saracosti*.

2 cups steamed wheat berries	1 bunch Italian parsley, chopped
½ cup sesame seeds, toasted	ripe pomegranate seeds
½ cup currants	coriander seeds
½ cup golden raisins	cinnamon and sugar to taste
½ cup almonds, chopped	

Love, care, and time are involved in this ritual preparation. Each ingredient is placed in a separate bowl and set on an improvised altar in the home. Candles are lit as remembrances, and blessings are asked. Vigil may be kept late into the night. The next morning the ingredients are mixed together and sprinkled well with cinnamon and sugar. They are arranged in quadrants in a large bowl, and decorated with a cross of whole almonds and a circle of pomegranate seeds. This symbolic offering is taken to church to be blessed by the priest. Usually large amounts of *coliva* are made; there is plenty to give to relatives and friends after the church service.

TARAMA CREMA SALATA

One dish shared with us this first day of *Saracosti* was called *Tarama crema salata*, a kind of fish roe mayonnaise. We were invited to watch the preparation in a friend's kitchen.

¼ lb. fish roe	2 cups olive oil
juice of 3 lemons	½ loaf dry French bread, crust removed

Tarama is made with a wooden mortar and pestle. First immerse the bread in water, leaving it to soak in a deep bowl. Put roe in the mortar with 2 to 3 tsp. lemon juice and 1 tsp. oil. Take a handful of bread, and squeeze out water. Mix into the paste in the mortar. Add all the bread in this manner. Working constantly, begin to add a little more lemon and a little more oil, 1 tsp. at a time. As mixture begins to thicken, watch carefully to avoid adding too much too fast; it is like making mayonnaise. Begin to check the taste after 1 cup of oil is used; stop when the taste and texture seem best. This is eaten as a spread on *lagana*, along with a handful of olives.

FOOD CONSERVES

"Many foods are made for conserve in Greece," we are told. Harvests of the sunny summer months are dried, or otherwise preserved and stored for the rest of the year. Grapes are pressed into wine, olives cured or pressed for oil, fruits dried in the sun, and milk turned into cheeses, or cooked with wheat and eggs for drying. These preparations of milk, wheat, and eggs are the Greek variations of pasta. They are made in the months when milk and eggs are plentiful, and days are long and sunny.

HILOPITES

Hilopites are tiny egg noodles. The name means "sun *pita*," and they are especially delicious on a rainy winter day.

The dough is made of 2 lbs. flour for every 10 to 15 eggs. Add enough milk to make a smooth dough that can be turned on a floured surface and kneaded with the hands. Divide the dough into fist-sized balls. Using a *pita* rolling stick, roll dough out very thin, as for *filo*. Place each *hilopita* on a clean, floured cloth and let it dry in a warm place. When partly dry, score the *hilopita* into ¼ inch diamonds with a sharp knife. When completely dry break *hilopita* into tiny pieces. *Hilopites* are stored in cloth bags in the cellar.

Cook *hilopites* in boiling water, as other noodles. Serve with melted butter or grated cheese or tomato sauce. *Hilopites* can be used as pasta to make *soupa avgho-lemono*.

TRACHANA

This is a kind of parboiled wheat. The following description of the preparation of grain and milk was given to us by Christos, our 80-year-old neighbor in the Peloponnesus:

"Do this in August when the milk is plenty. First, clean the wheat (remove chaff from kernels). And after, we cut the wheat by the mill (hand-turned quern). Don't make flour, but not fat, either; make four or five pieces to the wheat kernel. After, we put 4 kilos milk (almost 1 gallon sheep milk) in a big pot. Boil that. Then we put in 1 kilo wheat (about 2 pounds). The same time we boil the milk, we boil the wheat. But not much—little at a time. And leave the fire up. Make 'em round and round by the stick. And when the wheat is boiled all right—you have to make the taste—take it from the fire. Maybe after 1 hour. Take it off and cover with a lid to let stand 1 hour. After, when we look, it is pulled away from the side of the pot. Then it is good to take out. We take a clean cloth and make the *trachana* very thin. We put it to dry in the sun five or six days. And when it is ready, it is too hard to bite. Then we make it in tiny, tiny pieces like wheat again. We hang it in bags downstairs to store for all the year."

To cook, use a ratio of one part dry *trachana* to two parts liquid. Simmer *trachana* in milk with raisins and nuts for cereal. Or steam in water with chopped vegetables and eat with tomato sauce. Or make soup with egg-lemon sauce. Dried *trachana* requires only 10 to 15 minutes cooking time.

TRACHANAPITA

Trachana makes a thick, custard-like *pita*.

3 sheets *filo*	4 to 6 eggs
2 cups *trachana*, dry	1 tsp. cinnamon
4 cups water, or milk	¼ cup honey
melted butter	

Stir *trachana* into boiling water (milk will make richer, smoother filling). Simmer gently until wheat is soft and water is absorbed. Remove from fire. Stir in cinnamon and honey to taste. Add 2 to 4 well-beaten eggs. Roll out *filo*. Place 3 sheets in the bottom of a large baking pan. Brush each with melted butter. Pour *trachana* filling over the *filo*. Beat 2 eggs with 1 tsp. cold water. Spread over filling. A top layer of *filo* is optional. Bake in a medium hot oven at 350° for 30 minutes.

ARTICHOKES ISTANBUL

During the Byzantine Empire, Istanbul was united with Greece. Now it is Turkish. In spite of historical hostilities, the two countries have a common bond in food and share a cuisine which is equally loved by Muslims and Christians. In early spring we enjoyed artichokes Istanbul. The young artichokes, fresh from the garden, are cut with long stems, which are edible and delicious.

6 to 8 young artichokes	4 carrots
2 lemons	1 doz. whole pearl onions
½ cup olive oil	4 large potatoes
1 onion, chopped fine	1 bunch fresh dill, chopped
freshly ground black pepper	

Prepare artichokes by cutting off tough outer leaves, tops of other leaves, and the stems (cook these separately to eat hot or cold with a dip or in a purée). Wash well, and rub with a cut lemon. Set aside in cold salt water. Choose a large cast-iron or similar heavy pot with a tightly fitting lid. Heat olive oil. Sauté onion, and prepare the other vegetables: peel pearl onions, cut carrots into 1 inch pieces, cut potatoes into chunks. Add vegetables, except artichokes, to the hot oil. Stir for a few minutes—until potatoes begin to brown. Add chopped dill. Remove pot from fire and arrange artichokes among the other vegetables. Add juice of 1 lemon, salt and pepper, and hot water to barely cover vegetables. Replace lid and bake for 45 minutes, or until artichokes are tender. Serve hot, in plenty of its own delicious sauce.

Variation: Add uncooked rice to sauté mixture; steam with artichokes.

OLIVES

Olives are used in many ways. Straight off the tree they are not edible; they must be cured to remove a bitter substance known as tannin. Several methods may be used, each resulting in a unique type of delicious food.

OLIVE OIL

Olives used for making oil are picked green, before they turn reddish and begin to blacken. Any size can be used. The simplest way to harvest is to spread tarpaulins on the ground underneath the branches to catch the olives as they are plucked loose by pickers on ladders. Olives are then gathered and transferred into bags. Two or three people must work for several hours to collect all the thousands of olives from one tree.

At home, put the olives in a wooden tub and cover with clear fresh water. The water will turn dark brown as tannin is leached out of the olives. In 2 or 3 hours drain the liquid and replace with fresh water. Repeat several times daily, for 5 to 7 days, or until the rinse water pours off clear. With all the tannin removed, olives taste very bland. To make oil, drain thoroughly and put the whole olives through a screw press, like those used to make apple cider. Pits and pulp are strained out. Oil will separate and float to the top.

GREEN OLIVES

The olives eaten in the Balkans and the Near East are foods of real character, and can almost be considered a staple because of the quantity consumed. Olives are always served with salad or as a side dish. Often they constitute a whole meal with a little cheese and bread.

Green olives for eating should be a good size—about 1 inch. Slit each olive lengthwise 3 times, then place in a water bath to leach out tannin as for making oil. The final step is pickling. Put the olives in a wooden tub or ceramic crock, and cover with salt brine (½ cup salt to every gallon water). Let this stand from one to several days, judging by taste. After salting, olives may be pickled further in vinegar, sugar, and spices (proportions chosen to taste). Grape leaves may be added to keep olives crisp. Olives are stored in ceramic crocks. Salted green olives should be rinsed and thinly coated with oil; those pickled in vinegar are kept in the pickling solution.

BLACK OLIVES

The salty, wrinkled kind enjoyed by Christians, Muslims, and Jews.

Olives must be picked fully ripe, when they are soft and dark, resembling black cherries. Spread alternate layers of olives and rock salt in a wooden box. Let stand 24 hours. Each day thereafter mix the salt and olives thoroughly with your hands. Salt absorbs the tannin, producing a salty brown liquid that percolates through cracks in the box. Olives are cured in about 1 month, when they are very wrinkled and no longer acrid. Olives are then removed from the salt box, coated with a little olive oil, and stored in barrels.

SWEETS

Holidays in Greece are feast days calling for special food preparation, and the baking of breads and sweets. The most famous of these sweets is *baklava*, but there are seemingly endless variations and other equally delicious creations in this category. It is especially nice to be in a small village during a holiday, as the streets are filled with men, women, and children carrying pans of delicacies to and from the baker. (Most women have only large, wood-burning ovens, and prefer to take their sweets to the baker.) The finished products are beautiful to look at and wonderful to smell. Often we were tempted to follow their owners returning home from the baker.

BAKLAVA

This recipe calls for paper-thin, store-bought *filo*. One pound of these pastry sheets is enough for a large pan of *baklava*.

1 lb. store-bought *filo*	¾ lb. butter
4 lbs. shelled walnuts	approx. 3 doz. whole cloves
1 cup sugar	2 cups honey
2–3 Tbs. cinnamon	several helpers
1 cup sesame seeds	

Grind walnut meats with a mortar and pestle. Roast and grind sesame seeds. Mix nuts and seeds with sugar and cinnamon. Melt butter in a small sauce pan. Unroll *filo* and line the bottom of a large 12 x 15 x 2-inch greased baking pan with 4 sheets pastry. Brush each sheet with butter. Alternate layers of nut mixture with 1 or 2 sheets *filo* and butter up to the top of the pan. The top layer should be 3 or 4 sheets thick. Cut through the *baklava* horizontally first, then diagonally. Stick a clove into the top of each diamond-shaped piece. Bake 45 minutes at 350°. A paper can be placed over the top to prevent the *filo* from scorching. When baked, take *baklava* from the oven and pour on a syrup made of honey and hot water. Let stand 1 or 2 hours to saturate.

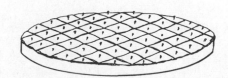

STRIFTES   Twists

Striftes are made the day after baking *Baklava*, using leftover nut mixture and hand-rolled *filo*:

Pastry dough.	¼ cup cooking oil
2 lbs. pastry flour	2 to 3 cups orange juice
1 tsp. baking powder	hot water as needed
½ tsp. salt	melted butter

Place 5 or 6 cups flour, mixed with baking powder and salt, in a large mixing bowl. Add oil and distribute evenly by rubbing flour through your hands. Make a well in the flour and add orange juice. Continue mixing with hands, adding hot water as needed to make a stiff dough. Turn dough out on a floured surface and knead smooth. Take a lump of dough the size of one pie crust. Pat flat on a floured surface. Roll out, following directions for *filo*. The circle of dough should be very thin and about 24 inches in diameter. Brush *filo* with melted butter and cover with nut mixture. Stiffly beaten egg whites can be added to the filling. Roll dough up and twist to seal edges. Prepare remaining *filo* and filling. Place the *striftes* in concentric circles in a greased baking pan. Brush generously with oil or butter. Slash outsides of the coils in 2 or 3 inch sections with a sharp knife. Bake in a medium oven for 20 to 30 minutes. Drip honey syrup over the top while *striftes* are hot from baking.

GALATOBOURIKO

Galatobouriko is a rich custard between thin layers of *filo*—a *pita* traditional to the carnival day before *Saracosti*.

½ lb. *filo*, or 6 sheets hand-rolled	10 eggs, separated
1 quart milk (sheep's is best)	2 tsp. grated orange rind
1½ cups sugar	2 jiggers fruit liqueur (optional)
¾ cup farina	1 tsp. vanilla
1 cup butter, softened	cinnamon

Heat milk together with half of the sugar until warm. Add farina slowly, stirring constantly. Add ½ cup butter; stir until melted. Remove from fire. Add vanilla, orange rind, and liqueur. Stir well and allow to cool. Beat egg yolks with remaining sugar until thick and frothy. Beat egg whites until stiff. Fold into yolks. Add farina-milk mixture and fold together. Grease a baking pan. Melt the remaining butter in a small saucepan. Place all but 4 sheets of *filo* (or 3 hand-rolled sheets) in the bottom, brushing each with melted butter. Pour in cooled custard and spread evenly. Sprinkle with cinnamon. Cover custard with remaining *filo*, each sheet brushed with butter. Cut through the top layers into square or diamond-shaped pieces. Bake at 350° for 1 hour. Meanwhile, prepare a honey syrup for the top.

HONEY SYRUP

1 cup honey	1 2-inch stick cinnamon
½ cup water	1 tsp. vanilla extract
grated peel of 1 orange	1 jigger fruit liqueur
3 cloves	

Bring ingredients (except vanilla and liqueur) to a boil in a saucepan; simmer for 15 minutes over low flame. Remove from heat, and add vanilla and liqueur. Pour cooled syrup over baked *galatobouriko*. Yum.

LUMBLIJE

A sweet spiced bread made in Yugoslavia for the celebration of November 1, All Saints' Day. Each woman bakes many loaves to give away among family and friends.

2 cups warm milk	¼ tsp. ground clove
¾ cup honey	grated peel of 1 lemon
½ lb. butter	dash of *Kruskovac*, vanilla, or anise
1 Tbs. active dry yeast	flavoring
1 tsp. salt	6 to 8 cups flour
½ tsp. nutmeg	1 cup chopped nuts
1 tsp. cinnamon	¾ cup raisins

Scald milk. Melt honey and butter in half of the milk in a large mixing bowl. When second cup of milk is cooled to lukewarm, stir in yeast. Mix salt and spices with 5 cups flour. Combine liquids and add flavoring. Stir dry ingredients in gradually. Fold in nuts and raisins. Place dough on a floured surface. knead until smooth, adding more flour as needed. Place dough in a clean, greased bowl, cover with damp towels, and set in a warm place to rise until it doubles in size. Punch dough down, knead, and allow to rise a second time. Punch down lightly and shape dough into loaves. Place in greased baking pans and let rise again for 1 hour. Brush loaves with melted butter and bake at 350° for 45 minutes.

VASILOPITA   New Year's Bread

"This is pure good, pure luxury," says an experienced *pita* eater. Luxurious and very rich.

6 to 8 cups flour	½ tsp. salt
1 cup fresh orange juice	1 tsp. cinnamon
2 Tbs. dry active yeast, dissolved in ¼ cup water	¼ tsp. nutmeg
	grated rind of 2 lemons and 2 oranges
½ lb. melted butter	almonds or walnuts
3 to 6 eggs, slightly beaten	sesame seeds
1 lb. sugar or honey	

Place 6 cups flour in a large bowl, making a well in the center. Dissolve yeast in water and combine with orange juice, melted butter, eggs, sugar, salt, and spices. Work this mixture in, folding in into the flour until well blended. Place dough on a floured board and knead smooth, adding flour as necessary. Allow dough to rise until double in size. Knead again lightly and shape into loaves. Place in greased pans and let rise again in a warm place. Brush with egg yolk and melted butter, sprinkle with sesame seeds, and decorate with whole nuts. Bake at 350° for 45 minutes.

It is the tradition to bury a silver coin in the dough before shaping the loaves. At midnight on New Year's Eve, the bread is cut by the head of the household. The one who finds the coin in his slice is blessed with good fortune in the coming year.

FIG. 24–Garden wheelbarrow and balance scale. Greece.

ROLLOS

Rollos is a special holiday sweet quite often made for name-day celebrations. Greeks do not celebrate birthdays. Instead, they celebrate each year on the day commemorating the saint after which they are named. Some names, such as *Christos* (Christ) or *Nikos* (St. Nicholas) are very popular. These name days are widely celebrated with much visiting, well-wishing, and feasting.

4 sheets *filo*	grated citron, or dried fruit
1½ lbs. almonds, ground to meal	and grated lemon peel
10 eggs	2 tsp. cinnamon
melted butter	½ cup sugar or honey

Separate eggs. Beat yolks with the sweetening. Add cinnamon, grated fruit, and nut meal. Beat whites until stiff. Fold into the mixture. Roll out 4 sheets of *filo* on a floured surface, brushing each with melted butter before laying on top of another. Spread filling along one edge, and fold the *filo* over to make a long roll. Continue rolling (and brushing with butter) over to the remaining edge. Place *rollos* in a greased baking pan. Slash through top in sections. Bake in a medium hot oven for 20 minutes. Drip honey over hot *rollos*.

KOLOKITHOPITA

Pumpkin pie! Rich with eggs and cream, this *pita* is made as a treat before the *Saracosti* fasting begins.

1 lb. store-bought *filo*, or	1 tsp. cinnamon
6–8 sheets hand-rolled *filo*	½ tsp. salt
2 cups cooked pumpkin	¼ to ½ cup sugar or honey
3 eggs, beaten	fresh mint leaves, minced
1 cup sheep milk (or top milk)	¼ lb. butter, melted

Mash pumpkin. Beat in all ingredients except butter until well blended. Adjust spices and sweetening to taste. Place 3 or 4 sheets of *filo* in the bottom of a baking pan, brushing each with melted butter. Spread pumpkin filling evenly. Cover with butter-brushed sheets of *filo*. Cut through *kolokithopita* with a sharp knife, making diamond-shaped pieces. Bake at 350° for 30 minutes.

FIG. 25–Rüzyarlar Köyü, Bolu, Turkey.

V. TURKISH FARM VILLAGES

OUR entrance to Turkey was not the standard overland route through Istanbul, but at the small port of Marmaris on the southern coast. We crossed the Mediterranean from Athens by ferryboats, meandering over the waters via Crete, Rhodos, and various small rocky islands between.* The day we docked was 8 April, clear and balmy; the fragrance of spring-time mingled with smells of the marketplace.

Debarkation was stepping from Europe to Asia. Our feelings combined romance with apprehension, as we had been briefed with many travelers' tales from this land. We took the fair weather as a good omen and began our travels as though Turkey were welcoming us with open arms.

Marmaris was calm, quiet and tidy. Along the quay was a bazaar; for sale were souvenir items from all over the country—including leather and woven goods, copper wares, ceramics, embroidery, and hand-knit stockings and hats from the eastern mountain region. Narrow streets leading off the market place were lined with small businesses. We visited the honey shop, the perfumery, the dried fruits and nuts shop, and the herbalist. We did not linger as we had a strong inclination to see the interior of the country. But we did have our first taste of Turkish food. From a street vendor was purchased a hot, fresh roll; long and flat and stuffed with a mixture of chopped egg, minced onion and tasty herbs.

The road from Marmaris follows the coast a few miles through a low, fertile valley, green with crops. Tall trees are planted as windbreaks at the edge of every field, and even this spring day a strong wind was blowing in from the ocean. Soon the road swings into the coastal mountains in the direction of Muğla, the provincial capital. These slopes are thickly forested with conifers; here the main activity is logging—for lumber and firewood. For the most part, these mountains are a wilderness, quiet and free of human activity. We passed a few rows of beehives set beside the road, and several low, arched cisterns (Fig. 26). The first inhabitants that we came to were a herd of camels, apparently without a herder.

As the forest thinned out to more open land, a herd of sheep bounded across the road. They were followed by a dark-eyed woman who was spinning wool as she tended her flock. We wanted to take a photograph, but had heard that picture-taking of Muslim women is frowned upon.

---

* During this period we travelled by motorcycle. The ferry between Rhodos and Marmaris is a passenger excursion boat. For the price of an extra fare we rolled the cycle aboard and tied it securely to a railing—one of the few practical advantages of touring by motorcycle.

Nevertheless, we decided to ask by bringing out the camera. We were surprised when she not only consented (Fig. 27), but gladly showed us her method of spinning. Photographing was accepted enthusiastically by the people of farms and small villages wherever we traveled in Turkey.

After leaving the mountains the landscape became flat, dry, and drab. We began to pass fields and houses of baked earth. Irrigation ditches ran along the road, and at each settlement that day great bundles of leeks stood in the water keeping fresh while waiting to be taken to the market in Mŭgla.

The wind blew up a rainstorm, so we stopped at a group of buildings for shelter. One was a grain mill, powered by water channelled along a wooden chute from a nearby stream. The miller invited us in to watch the torrent of water turning giant millstones (Chap. X). Then he took us into his home to meet his wife and share a meal. We sat on the floor at a low table, and ate together from one bowl of spicy soup.

When the rain cleared we travelled on, feeling more than ever that Turkey was opening her heart to us. In the coming weeks we had the opportunity to visit farming villages in many districts. In every instance, we were graciously accepted by local families, and asked to stay on as houseguests.

FIG. 26–Cistern. Mŭgla, Turkey.

FIG. 27–Spinning.

Fig. 28–View from minaret. Iscehisar Nahi, Turkey.

AN ADOBE VILLAGE

The province of Afyon (meaning opium) is the poppy growing district. However, in 1966 the Turkish government agreed to phase out opium production within five years as part of a financially compensated arrangement with the United States. The farmer's income there has always been minimal, and it is doubtful that he will receive the specified benefits. He is at the bottom of a long profit chain, growing a crop that requires a great deal of hand labor to harvest. Not much will grow in this semi-desert region. The other traditional occupations are weaving rugs (for export) and stone chipping (such items as troughs, basins, and building blocks).

We found Iscehisar Nahi at the end of a muddy side road. It was springtime and raining on the steppes of central Anatolia. We stopped to enjoy a rest and a hot cup of tea. The village teahouse was a large room, once painted aqua, with a solitary light bulb hanging from the ceiling. When we entered, the place was already filled with men who had come in from the rain. Everyone was very cordial, enjoying the opportunity to socialize in the middle of a working day. The proprietor refused to accept payment for our tea, as he considered us guests.

When the rain stopped, we left to walk around the streets. Soon we became fascinated by this village, which first appears to be a haphazard collection of impoverished earthen hovels, scooped out of an isolated hillside. As seen from above (Fig. 28), the rooftops look like so many plots of earth: there is little indication that there are houses below, other than a few chimneys stuck into the mud.

Being the first visitors in years, we received a particularly warm welcome from many villagers. We were invited in off the street to join a bread making gathering in an adobe bakery. The atmosphere inside was almost festive; the women socialized and munched on hot potatoes while watching their breads bake in the big oven.

While we prepared to leave the village, a neatly dressed young man approached us. He said it would rain again that afternoon, and that we should stay the night at his family's home. We weren't sure we understood, as he spoke only Turkish, but he was quite insistent. We were interested in meeting these people, and didn't want to refuse the chance of seeing the interior of their adobe dwellings. So we accompanied our acquaintance through the muddy streets that wind around a hill to the section called *Madres Mah*—'quarter of the theological school'.

The house that we came to, once whitewashed, was much like others of district, sharing one or two walls with adjacent buildings (Fig. 29). We were greeted by our host's mother, a plump, twinkle-eyed woman wearing an apron over striped bloomers, a multicolored blouse and vest, and a casually arranged veil.

The first thing after exchanging greetings was to remove our shoes, leaving them with others in the wide hallway. This central passageway serves several purposes in a Turkish household. Near the door was a kitchen work area. There was a narrow table with a small propane stove, and several shallow wooden troughs—constructed with their sides angling in toward the base. There were several sizes; smaller troughs were carved out of a single piece of wood. These troughs had many household purposes: making bread (Fig. 51), hauling laundry, feeding chickens, and other chores. Towards the rear of the hall was a large ceramic urn, buried in the tamped earth floor. This was for drinking water. In addition to these domestic uses, the passageway led to the animal stalls located just behind the living room. The latrine was located in an enclosed space between this house and a neighbor's (Fig. 29).

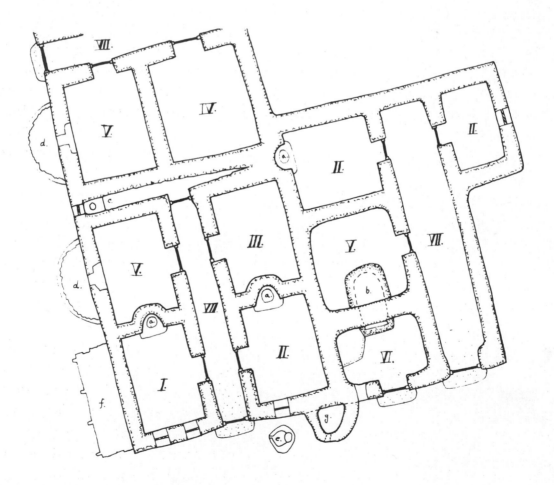

FIG. 29–A section of Madres Mah, Iscehisar Nahi. I. main room (eating and sleeping); II. bedroom; III. bedroom and storage; IV. storage; V. animal stalls; VI. bakery; VII. passageway and storage. a. fireplace; b. bake oven; c. privy; d. manure pile; e. stone basin; f. wood shed; g. chickens.

The living room was similar to many in Turkey. It was neatly organized and practically bare of furniture. The floor was covered with several layers of hand-woven rag rugs. Flanking the fireplace were two piles of embroidered pillows. Along one wall was an enclosed bench; in it was kept the family bedding, which was rolled out onto the floor each night. There was a sheet-metal wood stove, used for most of the cooking, and a fireplace built into the wall. Several wall nooks were created by laying a few adobe bricks lengthwise in the masonry, rather than by width. One of these nooks was a hole through the wall. On its ledge was placed a kerosene lamp which gave light to the living room and hallway simultaneously.

Towards evening, the father came home. He had already seen us in the village as we passed his feed and grain shop. He was pleased to find us, and indicated that we should relax and make ourselves comfortable. So while dinner was being prepared, we sat back on piles of cushions and attempted conversation with the family.

Family economy in this region is based on principles of self-sufficiency and communal cooperation. Approximately three-fourths of all Turkish farms are owned by their occupants. A small income is generally derived from cultivation, manual labor, or shopkeeping. Available resources are limited; everything is put to thorough use—e.g., poppy plants have several functions besides the opium harvest. Fresh greens are used as pot herbs. The seeds are ground into *hash kesh* (a delicious paste) for eating, or pressed to extract the oil. After pressing, the pulp is used for fodder or fertilizer. Dried stalks become oven fuel.

Almost every family keeps a variety of dairy animals, which are pastured each day in communal herds. It is a common sight to see groups of several hundred cows, water buffalos, sheep, and goats grazing together. The herders are often village women who knit, spin wool, or gather wild edible plants while they tend the animals. Squatting close to the earth in their full, colorful clothing, they look like giant wild flowers scattered across the countryside.

The arid grasslands found throughout most of Anatolia support little vegetation. Only certain breeds of animals can subsist on such barren land. Turkish cows give an average of 3 quarts milk per day. Though the yield is low, the milk is of high quality and extremely rich. Fat content averages 7 percent, compared to American cows' milk at 3 to 5 percent.

At Iscehisar Nahi there are two building techniques in general use. The simplest involves conventional masonry, of adobe bricks and adobe mortar. The only woodwork is the framing around doors and windows, and the poles supporting the roofing. These roofs are mostly earth, as is the floor, which is well tamped. In compression, adobe is very strong, but it cannot take lateral force. The main reason for a flat roof is that the weight is transferred directly downward onto the adobe walls. An alternative method of construction (seen in Fig. 36) is half-timber framing, in-filled with adobe bricks and other earthen materials. This calls for a large quantity of sawed lumber. But the resulting walls, particularly if well triangulated and tied together, are superior in strength. This is called for in any two-story construction.

Roofing poles are supplied by fast-growing trees, planted in a nearby irrigated field. During construction, these poles are overlaid with woven matting made of local rushes which, incidentally, make a very handsome ceiling. Above the matting is a course of stiff reeds, to which the earth is applied. To maintain drainage, roofs are never quite level. At the low points are long wooden spouts to keep rainwater from pouring down the adobe walls. Unfortunately, earthen roofing is unsafe in seismic areas (most of Turkey). During an earthquake, walls can fall outward, and the heavy roof may then collapse, killing the occupants.* A somewhat safer roofing is also seen in the foreground of Fig. 36. In this variation, the roof has a greater slope (approx. 30°). Reeds are thatched into a thick insulative layer. A thin coat of adobe is applied, often mixed with a stabilizer (such as cement in a mixture of 1:7), or finished with a coat of lime or plaster. This roof is lighter than solid earth (or conventional thatching that has become waterlogged).

FIG. 30–Ox-drawn "ard"—wooden plow. Sole, ears, and handle are an integral section of a tree. Eastern Thrace.

* A. F. Daldy, *Small Buildings in Earthquake Areas*, 1972.

FIG. 31–Waterworks. Bucket on well sweep is molded rubber.
FIG. 32–Stone watering troughs at an artesian spring.

33

34

35

36

FIG. 33–Mound on left is manure thrown out of a stall vent. Roof poles
support a stork's nest. Good luck! FIG. 34–A 30 degree angle
drains thatched roof plastered with adobe and lime. This construction is lighter (and safer) than plain sod foofing. FIG. 35–
Typical stone washbasins seen in front of most homes. FIG.
36–Two-story structure of braced timber framing, in-filled with
adobe bricks. Iscehisar Nahi.

A FOOTHILL VILLAGE

Traveling west between Ankara and Istanbul, we entered the province of Bolu. The highway threads its way along a mountain pass, then descends into a fertile valley almost at sea level. There, the road is flanked by wheat fields. Beyond these to the south are forested hills forming the base of Köroglu Tepesi, a peak rising almost 8,000 feet. Clusters of homes dot the foothill pines. This green belt is an exception to what we had seen in the arid parts of Turkey. We felt impelled to stop and visit the people of these farms.

Many small dirt roads join the highway, leading to small settlements. We chose one, and followed it through the fields and up a hill. The road became a narrow path, and our motorcycle began to slip backwards in the mud. There we stopped.

We were outside the large wooden gates of the four or five households of this *köyü* (cluster of homes). While still wondering what to do, we were joined by several cows, who came up the path with a young boy. The gates opened and a man came out to help drive the animals in. We were received just as naturally, and asked to stay the night.

Inside the courtyard (Fig. 37) we saw a large, two-story wooden house. The boards and timbers were hand-sawn and appeared rough and thick. There was one doorway opening into a wide L-shaped hallway. Here the floor was tamped earth, but the rest of the house had wooden flooring. To the right of the entrance was a storage area where household utensils hung from the walls and foodstuffs were kept in boxes and barrels. The end of the hallway was a lavatory, consisting of a sink and several brass water pitchers. Down a short hall to the left was a privy. To the right of the hall was a small room fitted with two wooden drain boards arranged one above the other, with spouts leading outside the house (Fig. 41). These were designed for cheese making, being used to drain off whey while curds hung in cloth bags from pegs in the wall above.

Downstairs was the living room where we met the family. Our host's name was Hamit. His wife was Minevver. The older boy (about twelve) was Yasar, the girl (eight) was Nezmiye, and the little brother (with shaved head and striped pants in the photos) was Iprahim. Hamit's mother, Rahime, lived with them.

The room was warm and full of activity. Fires burned in both fireplace and woodstove. Fig. 51 illustrates the brass water tank, fabricated to fit around half the stovepipe. The same photo shows Minevver sifting flour into a large wooden trough. Rahime was spinning wool with a drop spindle. And Hamit had the floor covered with wood peelings, as he was splitting saplings to make a basket. "Çalismak, çalismak" ("Work, work"), Hamit repeated, smiling broadly.

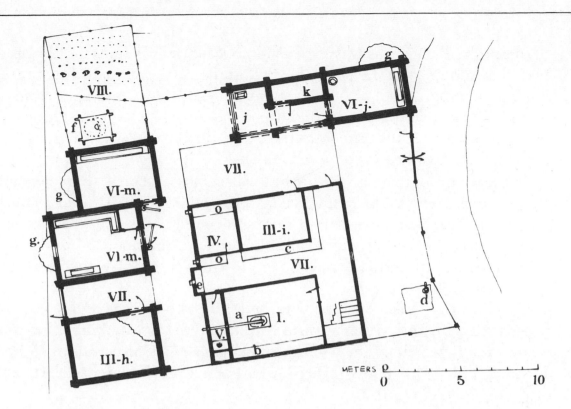

Fig. 37–Plan for a farmhouse and out building, with second floor of the main house shown below. Rüzyarlar Kōyü. I. cooking, eating and sleeping; II. bedroom; III. storage; IV. cheese making; V. privy; VI. stalls; VII. passage; VIII. garden. *a.* wood stove; *b.* enclosed bench; *c.* shelving; *d.* water pump; *e.* lavatory; *f.* bake oven; *g.* manure pile; *h.* hay; *i.* wood; *j.* sheep and goats; *k.* chickens; *m.* cows and buffalo; *n.* weaving; *o.* drain boards.

He then took us upstairs to the guest room. There was another small woodstove, and in a moment Yasar arrived with an armload of firewood. The furnishings included handmade carpets and a row of pillows along the wall. Two European style chairs beside a small table were set by the window. On the wall hung a color poster of Mecca.

There were three other rooms upstairs. One room was stacked with freshly milled lumber, a cross stick placed between each board for ventilation. On the wall hung a giant two-man frame saw, used to saw the lumber for this house. Hamit explained that it was now in retirement; his brother has a new motor-powered sawmill. He also told us that the boards he was seasoning had been logged by himself off the hill behind his house. More "*Çalismak.*"

In another room was Minevver's loom. She weaves household rugs and blankets and most of the fabric for the family clothing, including material for her bloomers. She also spins her yarn, and knits sweaters, vests and socks. (Before leaving, we traded a pair of her socks for a machine-made turtleneck sweater that she admired.) The third room was for storage and a nursery for two broods of young chicks.

These rooms opened off a wide hallway. Light and airy, this space made a good work area. At the end was a lavatory for washing, similar to the one directly beneath on the ground floor; to the left was the upstairs privy. Like most in Turkey, it was minimal—a hole in the floor, 6″ in diameter. Feces dropped directly down a boxed-in shaft to a pit in the earth. This was cleaned out regularly.

Downstairs, work continued in the main room. The fresh flour had become dough, and Minevver and Rahime were busy making hand-rolled pasta. Nezmiye helped the women make *macaronia* (Chap. VI, Fig. 52), and Iprahim played with his father's wood shavings. Yasar had left for his afternoon class in Quranic studies.

Just after sunset, the family stopped activities for evening worship. This *kōyü* was too small to have a mosque, and prayers were said at home. But the faint call of the *muezzin* from the closest village could be heard, beginning, "*Allah ho Akbar! Allah ho Akbar!*" ("God is greatest of all!") Then, removing from the wall several well-combed sheepskins used as prayer rugs, they faced east toward Mecca and offered prayers according to the tradition of orthodox Islam.

The next morning we had a chance to explore this small, hillside farm. Directly in front of the house was a courtyard, enclosed by a high wooden fence. In the center was a water pump (Fig. 49). The women built a fire on the ground, and on it was heating a huge kettle of water for washing clothes. This they do in large, shallow pans, squatting on the ground and scrubbing the laundry by hand. Minevver asked if we had any soiled clothes, offering the use of a pair of bloomers so Louise could wash her cycle-riding pants.

To one side and around the house were various outbuildings—structures built of notched logs chinked with mud, and roofed with tiles or corrugated metal (Fig. 44). There were stalls for the larger animals, including cows and water buffalo. A railed-in shelter was provided for goats, sheep, and chickens. An interesting detail, seen in Fig. 42, was the design and construction of doors to animal stalls. These consisted of two independent units, hinged from opposite sides, each being the full width of the doorway. From one side was hung a solid-board door that could be closed at night or during cold weather. From the other side was a gate of thin round poles, used during daytime to let light and fresh air inside. The

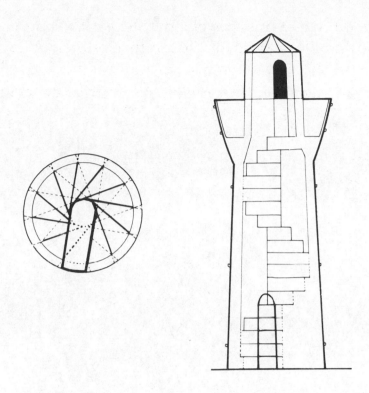

Fig. 38–In an Islamic village time is marked by five daily calls to prayer, chanted by the *muezzin* from a balcony of the minaret that adjoins every mosque. The call is heard in the pre-dawn morning, when the sun reaches its zenith, in mid-afternoon, just after sunset, and finally in the darkness before sleep.

hinges (also seen in Fig. 42) deserve some attention. The vertical style closest to the wall was extended beyond the top and bottom rungs. The lower end was sharpened to a point, and this pivoted in the concavity of a rock, set firmly in the ground. The upper extension swung freely within a natural wooden crotch, of which one leg was fastened to the side wall casing. Latches for these gates and doors were the sliding bar and lever types. Another detail, found in animal stalls throughout Turkey, was a thin slit in one wall used to facilitate manure hauling (Fig. 45).

In another shed, amidst carts, plows, shovels and other farming implements, we were surprised to see a bright red, diesel-powered tractor. As an explanation, Hamit related that he had spent two years working as a laborer in Holland. With his savings he had bought this machine. Leaving home to work in Western Europe is an experience common to the men of many poorer countries. This is, in fact, their most likely possibility of ever securing a sum of money. Often these laborers lose their earnings to swindlers or the high cost of living in foreign cities, or they return with a television set and other appliances hard to come by at home. Hamit returned with few souvenirs. He had worked to buy the tractor; almost everything else in his home remained traditional. *Çalismak.*

FIG. 39–Tile roof supported by an improvised selection of architectural
devices including a horizontal tie beam.

FIG. 40–Farmhouse and outbuildings. FIG. 41–Exterior detail of lavatory and whey drains at end of hallway.

FIG. 42–Overlapping doors provide an option of warmth, or light and ventilation.   FIG. 43–Interior of notched log stalls chinked with mud.

FIG. 44–Typical outbuilding construction. The carved wooden latch
includes a handmade lock: the door will not open if the smaller
crescent-shaped stick (seen fitted in the right side) is removed.
FIG. 45–Manure is thrown out of barn through slot between
notched logs.

FIG. 46–Rahime. Rüzyarlar Kōyü.

VI. *BISMI 'LLĀHI*

IN THE NAME OF *ALLAH*

IN Turkey the traveler is not a stranger, but an honored guest. Smiling faces extend a welcome, doors are opened, food prepared, friends and relations are called over, and the guest earnestly implored to stay a week or more. Language poses few problems with these people. *Merhaba!* we learned to say in greeting, and energetic sign language met most other needs. In fact, hospitality is a spiritual duty in the religion of Islam, and we found this a well-embraced practice.

Stopping at houses along the road, or accepting invitations from newly met friends, we were offered refreshments ranging from hot tea and full meals to garlics, freshly pulled from the garden. Often we attracted a gathering of twenty or thirty people, and our visit became a community event. Sometimes our audience was almost silent, and we sat together in a kind of nonverbal rapport.

TURKISH TEA

Although Turkish coffee is famous, tea is now the national drink. The decline of coffee drinking followed the deterioration of the Ottoman Empire; the loss of coffee-producing lands in North Africa and Arabia made coffee beans an imported luxury too expensive for the common householder. Tea, a government monopoly, was grown for the first time in 1931 along the coast of the Black Sea, and is now drunk copiously throughout the country.

Tea is drunk in the cafés where men meet to talk and play cards. Shopkeepers, tailors, auto mechanics, and barbers send out for tea to be brought to their customers. Delivery boys ride through the streets on bicycles, carrying trays laden with tea glasses. Tea is taken with meals and served as a refreshment. Some households keep tea water ready in a steaming hot samovar (Fig. 47) almost all day long.

Tea drinking is not only a social pleasantry; tea also serves to make boiled water a palatable drink. This is especially important in areas where fresh water is not always found, and tea is understood to be safer. Throughout Turkey, black tea is brewed very strong and served with an inordinate amount of sugar. The peculiarly shaped tea glasses hold only a few ounces.

TAKING *ÇAY*

Taking tea with a Turkish family is a ritual of household etiquette. It is a custom to offer refreshment, comfort and company, and the ceremony of preparing tea is a refinement in the art of making one welcome. This is not to say that taking tea is an elaborate, highly stylized event. The sophistication is not in the proceedings, but in attunement to the needs of a guest or traveler, and desire to honor him in the home. We met our tea hosts in cafés, on village streets, or along rural lanes—literally any time we struck up an aquaintance, we were certain to be invited home for tea. "*Çay, çay,*" our friend would insist, gesturing as though drinking, and already guiding us to some nearby or distant abode.

We could never refuse such generosity, and always followed along through narrow, rutted streets used by cows and sheep as well as people. We were taken into houses of no more than two rooms, bare of any non-utilitarian objects and sometimes even furniture. But at least a portion of the room was covered with woven rugs and piles of pillows used to make comfortable seats. Here we were given places to sit with our host while tea was prepared. The woman of the house heated water at the hearth while setting the tea table before us. This was a low round platform, or perhaps a large copper tray, holding tea glasses, sugar, and teapot. Strong black tea was brewed and served to everyone at the table. Sometimes a neighbor or relative joined, but other women and children in the room usually stayed apart, quietly enjoying the event.

In such an atmosphere of tranquility, simple bare rooms became the most gracious of teahouses. We felt as though held in a very special moment of complete sharing. There was little in the room beside tea, warm fire, and the circle of beings—all part of a ceremony. As *Americans* we experienced the luxury of the absence of material abundance. We sensed a balance in these lives—neither excess nor want—which left time and space to take tea and make friends of strangers.

A FARM HOME

We were on the way to the Black Sea coast, winding through the green hills near Amasya. It was dusk when we turned down a dirt road where we saw a few houses. Maybe there would be a camp spot. A farmer, finished with his day's work, was at the side of the road. We greeted him, "*Merhaba!*" He answered warmly and gestured us to stop. "You need a place to sleep," he said in sign language, and waved toward a large house, indicating that it was his. Incredulously, we followed him through the gate (large wooden doors in the adobe wall surrounding the yard) to a shelter for our motorcycle. Several children and two women quickly appeared, curious and excited. Our host shook our hands. His name was Necati. His twelve-year-old son, Chengiz, offered his hand, too. Then Necati brought a smiling woman forward—his wife, Samiye. We shook her hand, and then the hands of his sister Mujam and daughters, Fatima, Seniha, and Manife.

They unloaded our bags and carried them into the house. As it was time to eat, we all found places sitting cross-legged in a circle on the floor. We were given pillows and urged to make ourselves comfortable. We were eleven people, as the grandfather had appeared and a brother fetched from across the road. A large cloth was spread over all our laps, and a small, round table, 8 inches high, was placed on top of the cloth in the center. Mujam carried in a steaming samovar with a teapot perched on top and placed it near the table. Then the table was set with bowls of olives, cheese, poached eggs, and yogurt soup.

اللّه السمِ

"*Bismi 'Llāhi 'r-Rahmāni 'r-Rahim* ("In the Name of God, the All-Merciful, the Compassionate"), the grandfather asked a blessing for the meal before we began. We all shared the same bowls of food, dipping in with wooden spoons or with thick slices of home-baked bread. Tea was poured and refilled constantly by Mujam. It was she who brought the meal, refilled the soup bowl, and later cleared away the supper things.

As we finished eating, one of the neighbors and his brother came into the room. Following were his wife and three children. We shook hands all around and exchanged greetings. The newcomers were given tea, and the men lit cigarettes of home-grown tobacco. They were interested to see our travel maps and to learn our itinerary, which they traced enthusiastically with their fingers. The evening had become a special occasion. This welcoming party made us feel like long-awaited visitors being shared among close friends. Necati decided some entertainment was in order and began to sing a song, encouraging his daughters to perform a dance. Pots were brought from the kitchen to be used as drums and bright scarves tied on the girls' heads. And so, with much giggling, the dance began.

Fig. 47–Seniha and Manife dancing. In the foreground is a samovar—a special urn used for making tea. Hot coals are placed in the bottom, and water is heated in the surrounding jacket fitted with a spigot at the base.

When it was time to sleep, Samiye and Mujam carried in great piles of bedding from a storage room across the hall. Mats were rolled out and beds made on the floor for the whole family. We went to the room upstairs, where beds had been prepared on the floor for us also.

The family was awake early in the morning; we heard the children at dawn. As soon as we were up, they took us on a tour of the farm. We went in to eat about seven o'clock. Breakfast looked much like supper, consisting of *pilaf*, a spicy tomato soup, bread and cheese, and tea. Hot milk and sugar were also served. Wheat and milk are staples throughout Turkey, and the everyday diet is made up of endless variations of these foods: milk, yogurt, cultured milk drinks, cheeses, soups, bread, cracked wheat, *pilaf*, pasta, and more. These are served at any of the three daily meals. Soup in the morning and poached eggs for supper is as common as the reverse. Most cooking is done in a pot over an open hearth. Steamed grain dishes and soups predominate the menu.

After breakfast, when things had been cleared away and the room tidied, we went with Samiye and Mujam to get water at the village fountain. Water flowed out of a stone spring encasement and into a large tank. Women were gathered there to work and talk. Some were filling buckets or copper vessels to take home. Others were scouring their pots with sand or washing rugs, which they beat clean with heavy sticks. On a nearby woven brush fence, shining pots and bright rugs were spread to dry in the sun.

FIG. 48–Turkish bedding.

FIG. 49–Pumping water.

With their laughter and calling back and forth, the ladies were like so many brightly colored birds splashing in the water. Samiye and Mujam exchanged news with their friends, then filled buckets with water. These were hung on each end of a long wooden pole, which is carried across the shoulders. Mujam carried this load easily, with perfect balance and rhythm. (We found the swaying buckets caused one to stagger, and we could take no more than a few steps at a time. This gave the onlookers much enjoyment and laughter.)

MAKING DOLMA

Later in the morning we had a visit from the lady of a neighboring farmhouse. She had come to ask if Samiye would help make *dolma* (grapevine leaves stuffed with *pilaf*). We went together to her house. A work space was made in the main room by spreading a cloth on the floor to sit around. Then, a large round tray holding all the ingredients was brought and placed in the middle. Samiye and her friend worked together; one chopping, the other mixing to make stuffing. When the *pilaf* mixture was ready, they showed us how to roll it up inside a vine leaf. With three of us working, and a constant conversation running along, we soon had a potful of *dolma* ready to set on the fire. To clean up, everything was scooped into the cloth and carried to the kitchen.

DOLMA   Stuffed Grapevine Leaves

("*Dolmathes*" in Greece)

fresh or preserved vine leaves	**2 or 3 Tbs. tomato paste**
1 to 2 cups cracked or bulgar wheat*	**¼ cup pine nuts**
½ to 1 lb. ground lamb, sautéd	**½ tsp. salt**
1 onion, chopped fine	**dried chili peppers, crushed**
2 medium potatoes, diced	**1 Tbs. fresh mint, minced**
½ cup chopped parsley leaves	

Using fresh vine leaves, wash and drain. Sprinkle each leaf with coarse salt, and stack in a deep bowl with a plate on top to weigh down the pile. Allow the leaves to stand 24 hours. Immerse briefly in boiling water, drain, and set aside to cool. In a large bowl combine all the stuffing ingredients, blending the mixture thoroughly by hand. Place a leaf with shiny surface down on your open palm. Press 1 tsp. of the mixture in the center of the leaf; fold end of leaf over to cover filling; fold sides of leaf and roll carefully to make a tightly wrapped ball. Stuff all the leaves and arrange in layers in a pot with a tightly fitting lid. Pour 2 cups of water over the *dolma*; place a plate on top to serve as a weight. Cover with a lid and simmer over very low fire for 1 hour. Remove, drain and cool before serving. Serve on a platter with a bowl of chilled yogurt. A squeeze of fresh lemon is the essential complement to lighten and liven the taste.

PILAF

The ingredients for *pilaf* are the same as for *dolma* stuffing. However, the preparation and cooking method are different.

Heat 3 or 4 Tbs. butter or olive oil in a large frying pan. Add chopped onion, and sauté until transparent. Stir in ground meat, crumbling with a fork. Continue stirring until the meat is evenly browned. Add tomato paste, salt, crushed chilies and mint. Remove to a large mixing bowl. Heat more oil, if necessary, and sauté cracked wheat and diced potato until grain begins to change color. Stir often enough to brown wheat evenly. Add pine nuts. In a large pot bring to boiling 2 cups water for each cup wheat; add combined meat and grain mixtures. Stir well; cover and simmer over low fire for 30 minutes. *Pilaf* may also be prepared using rice.

STEAMED WHEAT

Served plain, or in another dish, steamed wheat appears at almost every Turkish meal.

1 cup cracked or bulgar wheat *	**salt**
2 cups water or broth	**4 Tbs. butter**

Use a skillet with a fitted lid. Melt butter, and add wheat, stirring to coat the grains. Add boiling water and salt. Stir and cover, then lower heat and simmer for 20 minutes.

Variation with chili pepper: Melt butter in skillet. Sauté finely chopped onion, garlic, parsley and scallions until golden. Add salt and ½ tsp. crushed chili peppers. Add cracked wheat and hot water; stir well. Bring to a boil, then cover and simmer over low fire for 20 minutes.

Variation with eggs: Steam cracked wheat (with or without vegetables) for 15 minutes. Uncover, and drop on eggs to poach on top. Powder with fine ground chili. Replace lid and cook 5 to 10 minutes longer, until eggs are set.

* Bulgar wheat (or *burguhl*) is partially cooked, or parched cracked wheat; commonly used in the Near East.

Fig. 50–Grindstones used to crack wheat for *pilaf*.

YUFKA EKMEK

In southern Turkey the women prepare a large flat bread resembling an elephant ear, called *yufka ekmek*, made from whole wheat flour (often freshly stone-ground, and slightly gritty). The dough is kneaded smooth, then rolled out with a long, thin rolling pin into a big circle (one-sixteenth-inch thick and 24 inches across). These flat breads are baked on top of a slightly convex steel disk, placed on a stand over hot coals in the fireplace.

The cooled bread, dry and crisp, is stored quite well in a stack on the pantry shelf. When *yufka* is to be eaten, certain preparation is necessary. The amount of bread needed is taken, and each piece is sprinkled with water. Dampened *yufka* is piled up, and the stack pressed and left to soften. To serve, each circle is folded into quarters or smaller. A pile is placed before each person around the table.

Yufka is very versatile. It is torn into convenient pieces and spread with butter or cheese, or dipped into yogurt or poached eggs. A man showed us how to fold *yufka* around one's thumb to make a tiny scoop, which he used to spoon up soup. Others wrap *yufka* around green onions and dip into salt or spicy dishes. At one home, a plate of chopped greens and a bowl of thick yogurt were passed around; each person spooned a portion onto the *yufka*, and rolled it up.

GREENS FOR *YUFKA EKMEK*

2 lbs. fresh greens (see *horta*) 1 clove garlic
4 scallions, chopped with stems 3 Tbs. olive oil
salt   1 egg, beaten

Steam greens over a small amount of water, covered, for 3 to 5 minutes. Remove from steamer and chop into small pieces. Heat olive oil with minced garlic and scallions in a frying pan. Sauté greens in oil for a few minutes. Sprinkle with salt and stir in beaten egg. Serve with yogurt as a filling for *yufka ekmek*, wheat tortillas, or arab bread.

YAOURT

Yogurt is an important food throughout lands where dairy animals or herding is a basic part of the economy and milk is a staple. Yogurt can be kept for several days without refrigeration; or even dried for later use. Although the goats, sheep, and water buffalo of the dry Turkish plains give relatively less milk than animals grazing on greener pastures, it is rich in butterfat and makes excellent yogurt.

Scald milk, then cool to 110°. (This is the temperature that is most conducive for the growth of acidophilus bacteria.) Add 3 or 4 Tbs. yogurt culture (ready-made yogurt) for every quart of milk and mix thoroughly. Pour milk into glass jars and incubate for 2 to 3 hours. A good method of incubation is to set jars of milk into a large pot of warm water (105°). Cover with a towel and set in a warm place; the temperature should remain fairly constant. This can be ensured by checking the water occasionally with a submersible thermometer. When yogurt is firm, move to a cool place. Cover with lids.

LEBNE Yogurt Cheese

A soft cheese is made by hanging yogurt to drain in a muslin cloth overnight. This is served plain, or flavored with garlic and onion to accompany meals. The cheese becomes very hard and dry if left hanging for a longer time. Then it can be used in cooking, either in soups or grated over grains or pasta.

KAMAK

Rich, thickened cream.

Kamak is made by heating whole milk or cream over low heat until it is reduced to one-sixth of the original volume. While cooking, the cream is aerated by ladling it above the pan and pouring it back. The result is thick as soft cream cheese. *Kamak* is allowed to stand overnight; in the morning it can be spread on bread for breakfast. This replaces butter in many Turkish households.

FIG. 51–Minevver sifting flour. In the foreground is a hot water tank set
on the woodstove.

YOGURT-WHEAT SOUP

Pour 4 cups boiling water over 1½ cups bulgar wheat. Cover, and let stand 2 hours, until all water is absorbed and wheat grains are light and easily separated. (Or, use 2 to 4 cups of leftover cooked *pilaf.* Any of several grains could be used, if they are not mushy.) Mix grain with 1 quart yogurt. Thin with buttermilk (or fresh milk) to desired consistency. Season with salt, minced garlic, and finely chopped fresh dill. Let soup stand 1 hour to blend flavors. Serve cold with whole, young green onions.

CACIK   Yogurt Cucumber Soup

2 cucumbers (or zucchini)   1 tsp. minced garlic
1½ tsp. salt   2 Tbs. olive oil
2 cups yogurt   ½ cup chopped walnuts (optional)
1 Tbs. fresh dill

Peel cucumbers and slice in half lengthwise. Cut pieces into ¼ inch slices. Place in a shallow bowl, and sprinkle evenly with 1 tsp. salt. Set aside for 15 minutes. Chop dill and garlic. Combine with remaining salt and yogurt in a deep bowl. Slowly stir in olive oil. Rinse cucumber in a sieve with cold water, drain and pat dry. Stir cucumber and walnuts into yogurt. Chill for one hour. A cool, summer evening soup.

MACARONIA

These are fresh Turkish noodles, made with leftover bread dough. Figs. 51, 52 and 53 illustrate *macaronia* being prepared for dinner in one of the homes which we visited. As for many tasks, the woman sat cross-legged on the floor while making the pasta. She worked on a large board which rested on her lap and the edge of a mixing trough, rolling out the dough in large, thin circles. *Macaronia* may be made from either yeasted bread dough or a standard noodle recipe:

3 egg yolks	1 tsp. salt
1 whole egg	2 cups whole wheat flour
¼ cup hot water	

Beat whole egg and yolks together until light and fluffy. Add other ingredients and mix well. Make a smooth dough. Cover with a damp cloth and allow to stand one half-hour. Divide dough into thirds. Roll sections out as thinly as possible on a floured board. Turkish women use a thin rolling stick, about ⅝ inch in diameter and 30 inches long. Roll the dough over itself around the stick, repeating from alternate edges to keep the circle even and regular. Once rolled, cut dough into 3 inch long diamond shapes. Fold opposite corners of the diamond around the end of the rolling stick and seal together, making a hollow cylinder of dough. Pull noddle off end of the stick. To cook, drop *macaronia* into boiling salted water for 10 to 15 minutes. Drain in a colander. Use as called for in noodle recipes.

MACARONIA CASSEROLE

hot cooked *macaronia*	¾ cup ground walnuts
1 cup finely grated cheese	4 to 6 Tbs. melted butter

To be authentic, use dried yogurt cheese. Otherwise substitute Parmesan or other hard cheese. Combine grated cheese and walnuts. Mix gently together with hot *macaronia*. Place in a deep casserole or baking dish. Pour melted butter over the top. Serve immediately, with cold cherry soup.

Fig. 52–Rolling dough for *macaronia*.

FIG. 53–Cooking *macaronia* on the open hearth. In the coals roast bagel-like rolls which were first cooked in boiling water.

CHERRY SOUP

Summer's abundance of ripe fruits is dried in the sun to store throughout the year. A cool, sweet bowl of fruit soup is a refreshing addition to the winter fare of wheat and potatoes. We had cherry and plum soups; other fruits could be used as well.

2 cups dried cherries (or other fruit) stick cinnamon
5 to 6 cups water honey to taste

Put cherries, water, and cinnamon in a large pot. Bring to a boil, simmer until fruit is softened. Add honey. Cover and let stand several hours. Serve when quite cool. This is a delicious breakfast soup.

HUMMUS

A zippy spread eaten with *yufka ekmak*, salads, or as a side dish. Protein balanced.

1 cup dry garbanzo beans, cooked ½ tsp. cumin, ground
½ cup sesame seeds, toasted ½ tsp. cayenne
1 onion ½ tsp. salt
4 to 6 cloves garlic juice of two lemons
¾ tsp. coriander, ground olive oil

Soak garbanzo beans overnight. Cook until tender. Pan roast sesame seeds, and grind finely with mortar and pestle. Heat olive oil in a skillet. Add ground coriander, cayenne, and cumin to hot oil and cook until spices begin to sputter. Add chopped onion and garlic. Sauté until transparent. Put beans and onion mixture through a food mill. Add sesame seeds, salt and lemon juice; mix well. Correct seasoning to taste. Allow *hummus* to stand several hours before serving. (Hummus may be prepared in an electric blender.)

VII. BAKE OVENS

AFTER the winter snow and rain, the unpaved roadways of Epirus (northwestern Greece) are all but impassable. By four–wheel drive we made our way along a trail of mud, rock and ruts to a village two hours' distance into the hills; the home of a friend's grandmother. The younger generation of this family have moved to the city, but the old woman cannot leave her world, and stays behind in an almost empty village. It is a world of ageless rhythms, time belonging only to the sun and seasons. The villagers are shepherds and farmers of small wheat fields and a few vineyards.

We found Grandmother in the courtyard carrying olive branches to her smoke-blackened bake oven. The living rooms were upstairs. There, she offered us places to sit around a wood-burning stove and insisted that we have homemade wine, and a meal of bread, eggs, and olives. The bread was baked in the oven outside; it was a smoke-flavored sour dough, traditionally made in these villages.

Her oven was similar to those still seen in rural districts. It had thick rock walls, and a domed brick ceiling (Fig. 64). The hearth, made of stone slabs, was round and had a diameter of approximately 3 feet. The floor extended in front to make a ledge, and was trenched at the doorway. The door was simply a piece of metal that could be placed in front of the opening.

FIG. 54–Bake oven with sheet iron door, wood peel, rag mop, and ash hoe. Greece.

Fig. 55–Adobe structure with two functions. Top half is a "dovecote"—a pigeon house built to collect droppings for use as fertilizer. Below is a bake oven.

BAKING LESSONS

Our source for many Greek recipes was Spitidoula, wife of the retired school principal of our village. Several times she gave us lessons using her brush-fire oven. We made breads and beautiful *vasilopita*, decorated with crosses of sesame seeds and walnuts (Chap. IV).

Unlike most ovens, which stand isolated in the yard, hers was built into an open-fronted shed (Figs. 56 and 57). The smoke hood joined the surrounding structure outside the oven proper (i.e., functionally, the chimney was not connected by a draft to the hearth). The overhanging roof provided weather protection, and storage for drying olive and orange prunings for fuel.

Baking with this oven was not difficult. It was heated with a succession of intense brush fires for 45 minutes to an hour before it was ready to use. Each fire was set and allowed to burn down to white ash; then the coals were spread around the edges of the baking chamber. Another pile of dry branches and sticks were stuffed inside and set afire. The oven was hot enough for baking after three or four of these short fires. Then coals were pulled into the trench with a hoe and the oven floor was swept clean with a mop of rags tied to the end of a long stick.

When the oven was sufficiently heated, a baker's peel (a long-handled, flat wooden shovel) was sprinkled with flour. Loaves were set on it, and shoveled inside. They rose in the heat and browned quickly—beautiful to watch. The door was left open for ten minutes, then covered for awhile, and reopened periodically for checking the baking and controlling the heat. Bread was baked in thirty to forty minutes. Then the door was left uncovered to allow the bread and oven to cool.

Fig. 56–Spitidoula preparing the hearth for baking *vasilopita*. Her oven is built into an open-fronted shed. Fig. 57–While baking, *pitas* are moved about inside the oven to brown evenly. Glowing embers are seen in the trench beneath the doorway. Fig. 58–Twin bake ovens.

IN TURKEY

One cold, rainy day near Afyon, we visited an adobe village. Almost everything there was built of sun-dried clay. In this village, the bakery was a specially built room, attached to one of the houses. The oven was shared by many families, and the women gathered to bake bread collectively.

Having been beckoned in from the muddy street, we entered a dim room, crowded with women and children. All were wearing stripes and flower patterns of many colors on the fabric of their full, gathered bloomers, patchwork blouses, vests, and wide sashes. Many wore embroidered head scarves, and some a chain of gold coins as a necklace. With all the color, laughter and excitement, there was definitely a festive atmosphere to this communal baking event. We were greeted by all, and pulled over to sit on a ledge at the side of the oven. This oven, sketched in Figs. 60 and 61, was very large. Only the front portion—the door and smoke hood—occupied the baking room. The fire chamber and hearth extended into an adjacent room (Fig. 29). A girl kneeled in front of the firebox and carefully tended the fire. The fuel was straw and small sticks, brought in constant supply by a child.

As the oven heated, several dozen oblong breads were set on an adobe platform to rise. When all was ready, the hearth was swept with a rag mop, and each bread punched down several times to flatten it. The woman at the fire, the baker, selected a peel and prepared to load the oven. Everyone moved back to the edges of the room, as the peel handle was very long. With a helper, the oven was quickly filled, and then closed with a metal door. Everyone smiled, and soon the room was filled with laughter and talking.

Minutes later the door was removed, and we looked in to see brown loaves ballooning in the intense heat. The baker woman rearranged the loaves deftly with her peel to make the baking even. The door was left open, and everyone drew in a little closer for a better view. Meanwhile, a small girl kneeled down to the smoldering fire, and filled her apron with potatoes that had been roasting there. These were passed around to munch on. Soon the first breads had finished, and these were taken out to cool. The loaves flattened quickly.

We were guests, so this baking became a special occasion—for the women as well as ourselves. One woman handed us a large chunk of fragrant bread and urged us to eat. "*Güzel, güzel*" ("good, good"), she said. The women gathered to watch us enjoy the bread. This was in the opium poppy district, and here we were introduced to a local specialty, *hash kesh*. A woman brought in dried poppy pods and slit them open to release tiny seeds into a stone mortar. With a pestle she ground the seeds to a paste and offered this to us for spreading on the bread. Poppy-seed butter! *Güzel*.

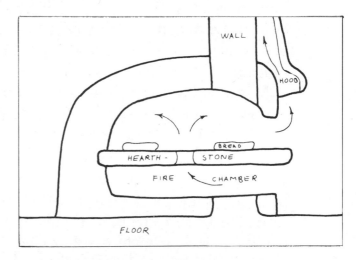

FIG. 59–Loading a straw-burning bake oven. A flame leaps through the center hold of the hearth from the fire-box below. FIGS. 60, 61–An adobe bakery. The fire-box extends into an adjacent animal shelter. Old straw is the fuel. Heat passes through hole in hearth-stone, and exits by external hood (supported by two short, con-cealed logs). Afyon, Turkey.

FIG. 62–Bake oven. Bolu, Turkey. FIG. 63–Mortar and pestle used to make *hash kesh*. Afyon, Turkey. FIG. 64–Interior of brick dome in a typical bake oven. Greece.

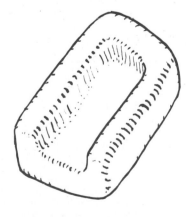

VIII. SPINNING*

OUR first encounter with hand spinning was a brief glimpse of the process performed by a peasant woman riding sidesaddle on a donkey along a rocky trail in the hills of Greece. We saw little more than a great cloud of fluffy unspun wool and a rapidly whirling ball of yarn. To our eyes, the appearance of yarn, pulled into the air like a spider's thread, was like magic.

On subsequent treks into the countryside, we frequently saw women spinning wool. Casual and relaxed at the craft, they spin while sitting or standing, talking with friends, or minding shop. The only implements needed are two simply fashioned sticks. A long forked stick is used to hold unspun wool. This is usually about 3 feet long, with three branches at one end. Well-combed wool is looped through the prongs and tied securely in place. The second stick is the spindle. It is 12 inches long, ½ inch thick in the middle, and tapered to ⅜'s of an inch at either end. The spindle is whittled smooth and round, and the top end is fitted with a wire hook. Some round weight, such as a wooden disk, or half a lemon, is used on the bottom as a flywheel.

While visiting our friend's grandmother, I told her of my interest in learning to spin. Before we left, she presented me with spinning sticks. Because it was midwinter, she had already spun her own wool, but she said

FIG. 65–Spinning in Greece.

* By Louise.

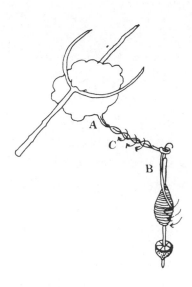

FIGS. 66, 67–Spinning lesson.

it would be possible to buy some in the marketplace. We found a shop, stacked to the ceiling with different colors and grades of wool, and bought a large bagful.

Equipped with the necessary gear, I was ready to learn the craft. Walking back from the market with wool and sticks in hand, we met an abundance of willing teachers. It seemed that every Greek woman who had ever spun yarn lit up in smiles at the chance to demonstrate her technique. I had only to hand over the wool and spindle to get a lesson.

Almost every woman had a different style for using the two implements. The wool-holding stick can be stuck through a sling and held under the arm; down the front of a vest, under the arm and through a belt, or between the knees in a sitting position. The important thing is a firm grip. The spindle can be worked in either vertical or horizontal positions. For the former, preferred for making strong, tight yarn for knitting, the spindle hangs freely on the yarn which passes through the hook on top. In use, the spindle looks like a top spinning in midair. In Fig. 66 I am holding the wool stick while our neighbor, Marina, demonstrates this method. The horizontal position involves turning the spindle with a flicking wrist movement as the unweighted end rests in the cradle of a half-closed palm. The spindle rotates clockwise while describing a counterclockwise circle in space. This method is generally used to make yarn for weaving rugs and blankets.

We carried our spinning equipment with us to Turkey, where our new friends found it interesting, but curious. In one household we were visiting, I demonstrated the Greek method to our hostess. She watched, then told me to throw the sticks away and try it Turkish style.

After a trial, I had to agree that her method was preferable. Instead of the cumbersome wool stick, Turkish women wrap a long strand of unspun wool around their left forearm and pull the wool free from the end of the coil (Fig. 27). The spindle is also more easily managed. Theirs is a thin stick, about 8 inches long, tapered and notched at one end. To facilitate its spinning, this spindle has four spokes formed by two intersecting flat wooden pieces, which are drilled through the center and passed over the spindle. These spokes are often elaborately carved or painted. In use, the spindle hangs from the yarn, which is wound in a ball around the spokes and then looped around a notch at the top. When all the wool is spun, the spindle is pulled out of the holes, and the spokes are disassembled, leaving a completed ball of yarn.

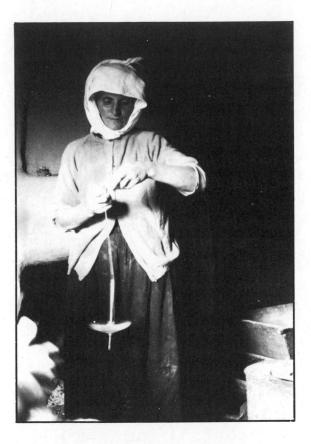

FIG. 68–Spinning in Turkey.

FIG. 69–Corn cribs. Turkey.

IX. BRUSH, REEDS AND WITHES

OVER-and-under weaving—or "randing"—forms the basic technique for a craft with applications ranging from basketry to fence making. The materials, generally foraged, must be fresh and green. These include split saplings, withes, reeds, rushes, and many varieties of grasses. Care in selection is important. For instance, saplings for splitting should be 2 to 4 inches in diameter, almost straight, and free of knots or imperfections. To ensure pliability, splits are usually used the day they are cut. If not, they are kept submerged in a stream or water trough.

In woven structures, weight is kept to a minimum. For certain uses, such as produce or grain storage, the inherent spaces provide air circulation to control temperature and prevent molds from developing. Woven baskets are generally very strong.

In a simple technology, wattle-and-daub construction is used to create walls of a peasant home. The same use of adobe plastered on a round, woven structure, makes a chicken coop. Many old beehives were essentially the same. Woven materials like willow wands can make an excellent corncrib. On a smaller scale, a hay basket is made, the right size and weight to heave onto an ox cart, or haul to the barn loft. In many areas are found woven fences, creating beautiful enclosures around fields, gardens and courtyards. Sometimes tree prunings are raddled with their mother trunk.

In Western Europe today randing is confined to basketry, used for both decorative and utilitarian purposes. Basketmaking is one of the few crafts that have avoided mechanization, thus providing a traditional livelihood for various isolated peoples.

THATCHING

Thatching, in one form or another, has long been used for shelter in many parts of the world. The idea is universal—to cover a framework with overlapping or layered plant materials creating a dry interior area. Very thick roofs can be constructed, and this provides excellent insulation for hot and cold climates. (Contrasted with tile or corrogated metal, which bake and freeze as the weather fluctuates.)

Thatching material is native vegetation, generally free for the taking, but sometimes grown specially for the purpose. In tropical countries broad leaves are commonly employed, often covering an entire structure. In much of Eurasia reeds and various types of straw are used. A roof of Norfolk reed (*phragnites communis*) may last over one hundred years. This is an aquatic plant which grows in English marshes in lengths of 3 to 10 feet. A properly thatched roof of wheat straw may last fifty years. Japanese thatching, using *kaya* grass or *yoshi* reeds, lasts 15 to 20 years. Other grasses, such as rye straw, thatch temporary structures such as shepherd's field huts and animal shelters.

In many areas thatching is the work of highly skilled craftsmen. As in other rural crafts, special techniques have been developed in various localities; and these employ different materials and reflect the needs and wealth of the users.

Beginning with harvesting, great care must be taken that thatch is not bent or crushed. One method is to first harvest grain ears using a hand sickle, then to carefully cut the reeds with a scythe and cradle. Another

FIG. 70–Thatching in progress, showing consecutive courses laid to achieve a smooth flowing surface. Material is combed red wheat. (Courtesy of *The Thatcher's Craft*. Published by Rural Industries Bureau, Wimbleton, England.)

FIG. 71–Trimming the ridge of a roof laid with Norfolk reed. (Courtesy of *The Thatcher's Craft*.)

approach involves hand threshing with beating flails. If the grain is not somehow removed the thatch will quickly become infested with vermin.

To begin, the material is gathered into parallel bundles with the butts level, and tied with straw rope. These bundles are then stitched into place between the roof furring strips and long thin runners using tarred twine, wire, or (in rural England) specially twisted wooden staples made of green hazel or willow. Thatching is done in horizontal courses, beginning at the eaves, with the thinner reed tips placed towards the roof ridge. In the more refined craft, successive courses pass over the runners, leaving no trace of the construction technique. This allows rain to shed along the surface continuously, rather than collecting above the horizontal runners and cascading from one layer to another. The roof should be pitched at least 45 degrees.

As work progresses the thatch is combed and beaten into place creating a smooth flowing surface. With some thatching it is customary to trim the bottoms of overhanging eaves (using a knife made from an old scythe blade). For the ridge a special technique or material is often used. In some cases the reed is tied in long horizontal bundles; or it may be held in place with wooden cross-spars.

The great problem with thatching is fire—originating on the inside of the house or from lightning. Many interior fires can be prevented by fitting metal sheeting around any fire areas or smoke holes. It is possible to saturate thatch with a fire-retardant solution before laying (this is mandatory in many parts of Europe). Thatched buildings can be protected from lightning by installing metal rods along all roof ridges, well insulated from the thatch and properly grounded. Thatched structures should be spaced rather far apart to reduce the danger of spreading conflagrations.

72

FIG. 72–Chicken coops. FIGS. 73, 74, 75–A flat landscape of grassland. Hollow "haystacks" are storage sheds and animal shelters. Hay is twisted into rope to secure casual thatching in place. A few miles away this type of construction using indigenous materials abruptly disappears. Sakarya, Turkey.

73

74

75

Fig. 76–Wattle-and-daub construction is simple and inexpensive. But safety precautions are not always taken: "The construction consists of wooden posts set upright about 75 cm. apart and interlaced with sticks or other material. One or both sides are plastered with earth. After some years the timber either decays or is eaten by termites and the wall is weakened. In this condition it will collapse in an earthquake of even moderate intensity, particularily if the roof is heavy. . . . If the use of this type of wall cannot be avoided the whole should be tied together and a lightweight roof should be used."* Another safety measure would be the use of a dry-rot and termite-proof foundation (soil cement or concrete). Also a coat of waterproof plaster could be applied to the walling. This example was seen in Haskovo Province, Bulgaria.

* A. F. Daldy, *Small Buildings in Earthquake Areas,* 1972.

FIG. 77–Pack baskets. FIG. 78–Gardening baskets of hazelnut splits, with solid wood bottoms, and bentwood handles. These get hard use and heavy loads. Switzerland.

Fig. 79–Goat enclosure. Fig. 80– Shepherd's field huts. Lower shelter is rectangular, having a roof based on a kingpin truss of rough hewn timbers. Thatch is hop straw. Greece.

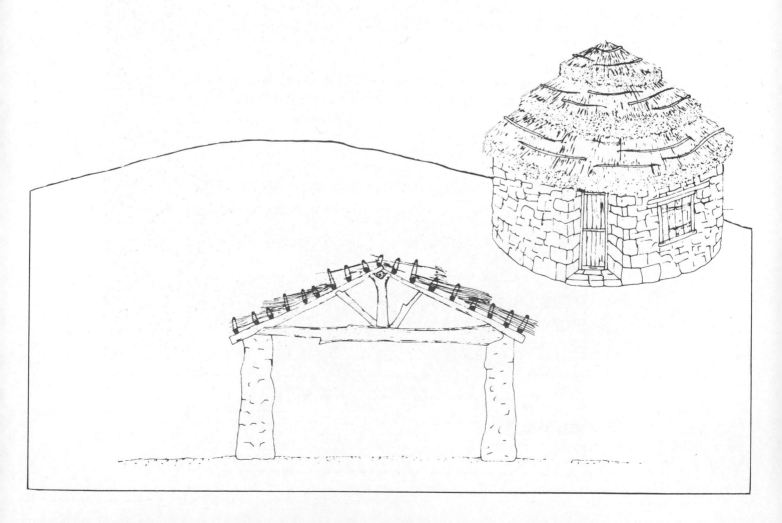

FIG. 81–Thatching in Switzerland. (Courtesy of *Das Aargauer Strohaus* by
Dr. Peter Felder. Verlag Paul Haupt; Bern, Switzerland.)

82

83

81

85

FIGS. 82–85– Rye straw thatching on animal shelters. Epirus, Greece.

FIG. 86–Thatched cap. Built on a light wooden frame, it is adjusted to height of stack by pulley at top of pole. Hay is pulled loose with a hooked stick. Holland. FIG. 87–Storage shed. Lolland, Denmark.

FIG 88-Thatching with long straw, Huntingdonshire, England (Courtesy of *The Thatcher's Craft*.) FIG. 89-Rural cottages. Lolland, Denmark.

FIG. 90–Field structure located on a sub-arctic plain. Log grid holds down thatch subjected to extreme conditions of a long winter season. Notched construction has been continued through the gable, creating a very strong roof capable of withstanding heavy loads. (Generally, log structures end the notched construction at base of the gable, utilizing conventional roofing techniques of vertical supports, ridgepoles and rafters.) As it is fully tied together, this structure could be used in earthquake areas. Vääsanlaani, Finland.

FIG. 91–Farm building with thatched roof and enclosed yard. Bosnia-Hercegovinia, Yugoslavia. FIG. 92–Woven fencing. Samsun Estuary, Turkey.

FIGS. 93, 94–Seasonal alpine fencing; removed before snowfall in avalanche areas. Canton Graubünden, Switzerland.

FIGS. 95, 96–Fencing at Lilliehammer Open Air Museum, Norway.

FIG. 97–Wood seasoning. Larger logs are piled in a "V", bottom ends crisscrossed. Smaller poles and saplings are stacked in the resulting crotch. This system promotes air circulation and prevents rot. FIG. 98–Withe-tied fencing. Gudbrandsdalen, Norway.

Fig. 99–Anti-erosion measures. In a natural gully, horizontal members are notched into longitudinal logs to prevent loose rock from washing away. Fig. 100–Retaining wall constructed of horizontal logs notched into pilings driven into the hillside. Switzerland.

X. GLIMPSES OF UNIVERSAL ENERGY

THERE is something special about windmills and waterwheels. They are energy centers, attuned to the elements, and peacefully carrying on everyday magic. Wind or water passes through blades; machinery is put into motion; whole grain becomes flour; this becomes bread, which is in turn energy. There is minimal cost for this motion. More important, the machinery is nonpolluting, and there is still wind and water when all is done. We were always attracted to these kaleidoscopes of energy but did not attempt a study of the subject. The following is included as examples of possible applications of free power resources.

FIG. 101–The broad tableland of Lassithi, Crete, is extensively irrigated by hundreds of windpumps turned by adjustable cotton sails. Formerly the supporting pylons were wood, but most have been replaced with angle iron. The extremely light wooden spars are strengthened by a three-dimensional network. Lines are rigged around the perimeter of the sails, and fore and aft to a "bowsprit" and weather vane—which keeps the sails facing directly into the wind. Turning speed may be regulated by the number of sails rigged; the pattern must be symmetrical. Water is collected in a cement cistern.

FIG. 102–Windpump near Neapolis, Crete. Base of the stone pylon is
hollow to house the pumping mechanism.

103

FIG. 103–Throughout Turkey waterpower is widely used to drive flour mills. A mill located on the roadside near Dinar was supplied with water carried over arid wasteland by a rickety wooden aqueduct. FIG. 104–The miller was happy to demonstrate its use. By means of a lever, the tub wheel was lowered into the millrace. As the upper stone began to turn, grain was fed through the funnel and into the eye of the millstone. Flour came out the spout and emptied into a large bin. Showing typical Turkish hospitality, the miller then invited us to stay for a meal with his family, at which we ate *yufka ekmek* made from freshly ground flour. FIG. 105–A horizontal water wheel of welded steel (not installed).

104

105

FIG. 106–Amid the wheat fields of Bolu province, we found waterpower very much in use. One miller had two large mills working and a third under construction. We watched as he fabricated the timber framework to hold the new grindstones. His mills were equipped with swinging cranes for lifting the stones, which require dressing every two weeks. At this place we also saw a water-driven clothes washing machine. The mechanism worked by means of an under-shot waterwheel turning a crank rod attached to a grooved timber sliding back and forth within a wooden trough. Clothes to be washed are put between these moving parts. The device was well-engineered, with carved wooden channels constantly feeding water over the hardwood bearings and through the washing apparatus. The inventor laughed as he explained that the machine was used to wash only heavy work pants.

106

107

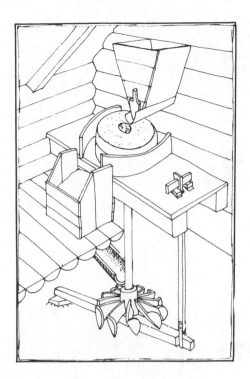

108

FIGS. 107–109–Along a remote valley road in the mountains of Makedonija, Yugoslavia, we came upon a number of flour mills built directly over a rushing stream. The horizontally mounted tub wheels were carved like wooden propellers. The mill houses were neatly built of notched timbers, with steeply pitched roofs and clapboard shingles. The same basic design was also seen in a flour mill built in the Middle Ages, now installed at the *Norsk Folkmuseum*, in Oslo.

FIG. 110–The magnificent windmills of Northern Europe were made to turn three sets of grindstones. The cap and gearing rotate on an elevated track so that the blades may be faced into the wind. This mill, seen in Denmark, uses cloth sails stretched over wooden battens.

Fig. 111–Storage houses placed on posts as a protective measure against mice and other vermin. Numedal, Norway.

XI. A GALLERY of SCANDINAVIAN ARCHITECTURE

OUR travels in Scandinavia followed seven months of rural exploration through the Balkans and Near East. At the time, we did not feel attached to the idea of returning home, but we wanted very much to settle. We felt that Norway or Finland might provide ideal opportunities for immigration. These countries are rather large, of low population density, and fairly prosperous. They are considered socially and politically liberal. Our hope was to find available land in a farm community along a hypothetical belt existing between rich agricultural districts of the warmer south and the vast, seemingly endless north.

We learned that many small farms are being abandoned, especially in Norway. Life is hard, income too low. Often, no local schools are available. When children grow up, they generally move away, and leave their parents to carry on alone. Certain government policies have been adopted to make farming more prosperous. However, these laws tend to encourage ever-expanding growth and mechanization of large farms, rather than encouraging small communities, which we consider a basic cultural resource of a healthy society. When a farm is up for sale the adjacent farmers have first option to purchase, which is done through a government contract or concession. For a newcomer, it is necessary to receive a consensus from the surrounding neighbors. The government makes loans and many kinds of subsidies available to farmers (even newcomers and, theoretically, foreigners). This means it is unlikely that a desirable farm would not be bought by an established neighbor.

We investigated legal aspects of immigration to Norway. In Oslo we were directed to three different official buildings before we found the correct, rather obscure, office. Apparently there are few immigrants, although men from southern European countries often come to Scandinavia for work. The solitary clerk explained that to become citizens we would have to maintain residence for seven years. During that period there would be no papers to file. However, if we wanted jobs, we would need work permits. It would be necessary to obtain a Residence Permit from the U.S. Embassy. After becoming citizens, men are drafted into the army.

FIG. 112–Detail of grain loft seen in FIG. 111. Built 1778.

As for land, the best farmland and the most prosperous farmers are in the environs of Oslo. Our explorations avoided the very rainy Bergen area as well as the far north, taking us up and down the Numedal and Gudbrandsdalen valleys in the central part of the country. Here land is good and the scenery beautiful—green, forested hills descending to bounteous farms along blue, rolling rivers. Weather is comparable to more southern latitudes. Summer days are warm and very long. At the 62nd parallel, sunset is late at night in June and July. The sky is never darker than dusk, so a farmer can work five or six extra hours in his fields and still go fishing. Sunrise is about 3:00 A.M. (True Midnight Sun begins at 66½° where the sun never sinks below the horizon on summer solstice. North of the Circle the Midnight Sun begins earlier and lasts longer.) It is these exceptionally long hours of daylight that are responsible for the abundant produce grown in the short season. Conversely, winter is cold and long—a time of darkness.

The farmland we visited was being used productively. We did not make a thorough search for land to buy as we were never tempted by what we saw. We made our judgment based on personal needs, which include aesthetics and interaction with people. We believe it is important to participate in a community . . . in its schools, economy, and social life. In rural Norway we felt little sense of community; towns seem to exist mainly to facilitate highway traffic and consumer demand. We noticed a conspicuous lack of centers, meeting halls, inns or taverns. Rather, stores are strewn along roadsides without social relevancy. Farmsteads are isolated, and often decked with aluminum lawn furniture, plastic household accessories, and fields of cheap bungalows for renting to summer vacationers.

Working to offer an alternative is an expanding movement of young humanistic and ecology-oriented activists. Stirrings began at the college centers of Oslo, Bergen, and Kristiansand. Interest is both practical and theoretical. A special organization (PAG) has been formed to help people buy and live on small farms. We spoke to some of their organizers, who said there were some 200 active members. PAG purchased five farms in 1972 and hoped to have over one hundred in the next few years. Although most available land is hard to farm commercially, it is often fine for homesteading. PAG favors group endeavors, as such work is difficult. The farms are generally in the fertile, rainy south and west coasts, and some rather remote northern spots. (Mountain plateaus between inland valleys are for the most part semi-arctic, rocky and unusable.)

Evidence that Scandinavian farms were capable of supporting generations of hearty farmers is exhibited in extensive open air museums of folk culture. The ones at Oslo, Stockholm, and Helsinki contain hundreds of beautifully reconstructed farm buildings, many complete with furnishings. In older times, Scandinavian farmers built with a style and boldness that makes credible their seagoing relatives' adventures in the far Atlantic. The work is often massive, yet with fine lines; such particular details and period styles could be accomplished only by proud men.

The seed of Scandinavian rural building was developed in the Middle Ages; distinctive qualities remained in the craft through the eighteenth century. Rural farmsteads combined primitive with the elegant. These structures provided few comforts or luxuries. The older constructions were dark (generally without windows) and often soot-blackened, as the fireplace was generally an open pit in the center of the main room. Cooking was done in iron pots on legs, or in kettles suspended by an adjustable trammel or S-hook. Until the eighteenth century, many farm structures were built with tamped earth floors.

Buildings were elegant as a result of the builders' sensitivity and respect for both environment and craft. Long, cold winters require sound construction. Logs being the fundamental material, these craftsmen became highly skilled axmen. The degree of accuracy in fitting members was exceptional. Generally the plainest type of notching was used, but great care was taken. An interesting variation was the hewing of huge logs into giant ovals. Using this technique, as few as three log courses were sufficient to build one story.

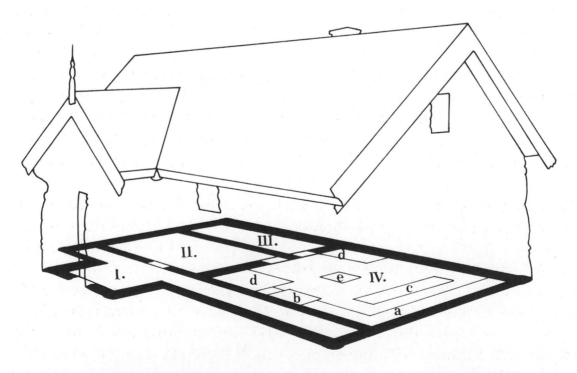

FIG. 113–*Stue* (farmhouse) with tripartite floor plan and outer gallery. I. outer gallery; II. storage room; III. mill room; IV. living room. *a.* benches; *b.* chest; *c.* table; *d.* beds; *e.* fire pit.

FIG. 114—Exterior of *slue* seen in Fig. 113. Numedal, Norway.

The *slue* (living quarters) was commonly built on a tripartite plan (Fig. 113). This design consisted of three ground-floor rooms, not counting the outer gallery. The small entrance room was most useful in wintertime, as it kept cold outside air from entering the rest of the house. The main room combined space for cooking, eating, sleeping, and other activities. Ceiling rafters were used for drying, and as storage racks for clothes, tools, smoked meats, bread, etc. Large quantities of flat dry bread were kept, as baking was done but twice a year. There was also a small storage room containing foodstuffs and a quern for grinding grain (Fig. 119). Upstairs was a loft where children slept, reached by a ladder or steep staircase located in the entrance room or gallery (Fig. 129).

Furnishings were simple, sturdy, and functional. Design and size made use of large sections of wood. Sometimes unusual tree growths were incorporated into construction: i.e., chairs carved out of single log chunks. Traditional dining tables were made of thick slices from the centers of large trees, and reached 12 to 20 feet in length. Smaller tables were often hinged against a wall when not in use. Benches were generally attached along one or two walls. Beds, often with corner posts reaching to the ceiling, and enclosed with heavy curtains, were built into corners of the living room. These were short and wide; presumably, these tall people slept curled up or partly upright. Goose-feather quilts were used for extra warmth.

On the typical farm were several outbuildings, constructed some distance apart as a precaution against loss from fire. Shown in Fig. 128 is a barn with hay and grain lofts. A ramp leads to the center room, which serves as a threshing floor. The two wings provide storage space for grains and hay. Stalls are located on the ground level. In many areas vermin-proof storage houses were built. These were set on short stilts, often of particularly beautiful design and craftsmanship (Figs. 120, 121).

Development of the outer gallery—an enclosed porch running around the front and sometimes sides of *stues*, barns and lofts—was a unique and highly successful architectural device. Made of planks, the gallery shields exterior stairways, provides storage for tools, insulates the interior rooms, and protects structural members from wear of the elements.

Many farms, particularly in Finland, included a sauna house among the outbuildings (Fig. 130). This was a windowless log hut with an exceptionally low ceiling. A fire was built within a chamber of basaltic rocks piled to make a rough dome. The rocks retained heat, and the bath began after the fire had burned down to coals and smoke had filtered out. People sat on plank benches above the fire and poured water over the hot rocks to create steam. Sauna huts were also used as smokehouses to cure meats and dry grain to make malt for beer.

FIG. 115–*Stue* details. On left is a walking-trainer and an infant's swinging cradle. Finland.

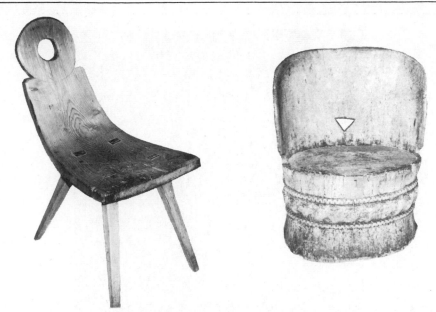

FIG. 116–Chairs. Left: *Seurasaari* (open air museum), Helsinki. Right: *Norsk Folkmuseum*, Oslo.

Early houses displayed a variety of roofing techniques. The most colorful was sod, having a rich growth of green turf and wild flowers during the warmer months. Sod is an effective insulation in hot and cold weather. There was no lack of stout logs to support such a weighty construction. Waterproofing was accomplished by layers of bark beneath the sod. In Finland a roof style that used tree trunks 8″ to 12″ in diameter was developed. An extremely obtuse V-groove was cut down the full length of each log, which was then perpendicularly attached to the superstructure. These were placed alternating V-up and V-down. This sturdy roofing was used on houses, lofts, sheds and field huts. Figs. 126–128 show the use of slate roofing—both large, random slabs and precisely cut tiles. The stave church at Al (Fig. 137) is an example of particularly beautiful slate work, glittering many colors in bright sunlight. The famous stave church from Gol, now in the *Norsk Folkmuseum*, is roofed with elegant, hand-carved wooden shingles (Fig. 135). Plain wood shingles were used on many farmsteads. Thatching is to be found in Finland even today. A typical example is the field storage shed at Vaasanlääni, one of hundreds still in use (Fig. 90).

We did prefer to see buildings in their original sites, and many still sit in beautiful valleys where the museum pieces come from. The old farms are a pleasure to see, but their owners have often found it expedient to replace sod or slate roofs with tiles or corrugated metal, or to paint the ancient weathered wood bright red. Old buildings are often allowed to fall into disrepair. Like the Lord Elgin Marbles removed from the Acropolis and now exhibited in The British Museum, many of these rural masterpieces would have rotted away in obscurity if not otherwise preserved and maintained in the folk museums.

FIG. 117–Outer gallery detail showing handmade cleats. Seurasaari.
FIG. 118–Main room of a *stue* showing continuous wall benches,
typical short bed, and table that folds against the wall when not in
use. The window is not original.

FIG. 119–Farmstead mill room. Quern used to grind meal from grains.
The handle, an iron rod, fits into a hole in an upper timber.
Seurasaari.

120

121

FIGS. 120, 121–Post details. Norsk Folkmuseum.

FIGS. 122, 123–Doorways of small huts used by hunters and loggers.
Interior furnishings are a central fire pit and box beds.
Lilliehammer Folkmuseum.

FIGS. 124, 125–Forest hut with sod roof. Bark liner laid against edge boards retains sod. Rocks are used to help shape bark. Lilliehammer.

Figs. 126–128–Slate roofing in Gudbrandsdalen, Norway. In Fig. 128 the ramp leads to a threshing floor. Grain and hay storage are on either side.

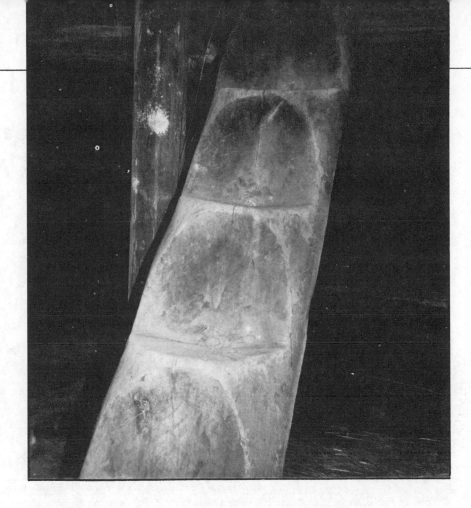

Fig. 129–Carved stair-ladder. Seurasaari. Fig. 130–Interior of a sauna house. Seurasaari.

FIGS. 131, 132–Outbuilding from Savo, Finland. Upper floor serves for summer sleeping quarters, lower floor for storage. Seurassari.

FIG. 133–Bearproof meat storehouse from Lapland. FIG. 134–A fox trap from Lapland. The carved board, approximately five feet long, is driven into the earth. A piece of meat is skewered on the top fork. When a fox leaps for the meat his front paws catch in the side forks; and there he is when the hunter returns. Seruasaari.

FIG. 135–Stave church from Gol, Hallingdal, built about 1200 A.D.
Norsk Folkmuseum.

137

136

138

FIGS. 136–138–Details from stave church at Al, Hallingdal, Norway.

XII. ALPINE ARCHITECTURE OF SWITZERLAND

THE materials, construction, and design of all architecture are intricately related within any cultural matrix. In folk architecture, we see a closeness of these elements to people. Materials are generally drawn from within the proximity of the building site. Structures are owner-built, or a specialist may be used. Sometimes construction (or a phase of construction) may be a community project. Design almost always follows local patterns, but individualism is not unknown.

FIG. 139–Notched half-logs represent a link between construction with round logs and more sophisticated square timbers. Advantages in using half-logs include economy, ease in handling, and the resulting smooth interior siding. Dated 1585. (Original wood shingles have been replaced with a synthetic product.) Canton Bern.

Fig. 140–*Bauernhäuser* constructed on an avalanche slope. Canton Graubünden.

Swiss workmanship is renowned for quality, precision, dependability, and longevity—all aspects of alpine architecture. The resources available to the traditional *Zimmermeister* (master carpenter) were wood, stone, and water. At work he used skills acquired through apprenticeship and experience, these being techniques handed down generation upon generation during the centuries that this architecture developed. His problems included the fact that he would often be working in an isolated location. Whatever was built would have to endure many seasons. Construction techniques had to include provisions for alpine earth movement, avalanche, and extreme temperature variance. Lacking in iron ore and fossil fuels, metal work was kept to a minimum (mostly locks and hinges).

Building began with felling local trees. This was done in wintertime, preferably during a waning moon. Draft horses pulled logs to a sawmill or to the construction site over snow. There was no damage to the fragile alpine ground structure. In spring, stumps were removed for firewood. Walking in the alpine woods today, one sees few signs of logging activity, although these forests have been harvested for hundreds of years. Reforestation is conscientiously practiced, and there are few ruts caused by erosion.

With the trees felled, bark was stripped as soon as possible to prevent rot and insect infestation. At a water-driven sawmill, wood was cut into timbers approximately 5″ wide and 8″ to 12″ high. Timbers were stacked crisscross fashion, with a 5″ space between each, and allowed to air-season three years. Some wood was cut into lumber 2″ thick for flooring, and 1″ thick for making furniture, doors and window shutters. This lumber was seasoned one year. If no mill was available, logs were hand hewn into rectangular timbers with broad ax and foot adze.

During our Swiss travels we had the opportunity to stay in some of these buildings. For ten weeks we lived with an alpine *Senn* (herder and cheese maker). His *Alpenhütte* (Fig. 165) was built between 250 and 300 years ago. Armin proudly showed us that the oldest ax-hewn timbers were exceptionally smooth, whereas on the undersides of the mill-sawn floorboards one could see marks from the passing saw blade. These oldest timbers were found only in one section, the *Alpenhütte* having undergone reconstruction over the centuries. Armin's father bought *Chirel Alp* in 1910, and at that time the barn section was at least 500 years old. As this part was in poor condition, a *Zimmermeister* was hired to construct new stalls on the old foundation. Some of the ancient timbers remain in use, but most were cut new and seasoned at the site. This location had no access by road; a horse was used to haul a small gasoline-powered sawyer's rig to the job.

The typical interlocked construction of these alpine buildings was a sophisticated version of the familiar notched log cabin (Fig. 148). Designs developed gradually and displayed a variety of styles reflecting local and cantonal customs as well as the owner's needs and wealth. Notching was often combined with grooved post and tongued lintel and siding work, resulting in flush appearance in the interior walls and around doors and windows (Fig. 149). Nails were not needed.

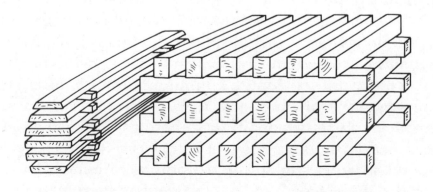

Fig. 141–Seasoning boards and timbers.

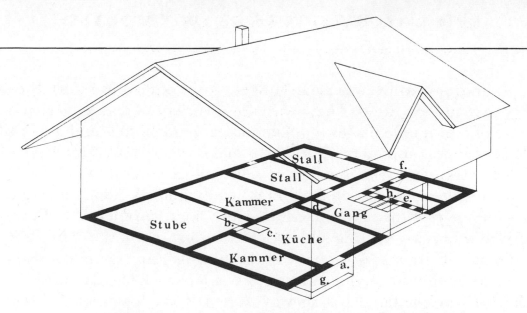

Fig. 142–*Bauernhäus* of the Berner-Oberland (constructed about 1830). On the ground floor are living quarters for the family, stalls, and storerooms. The second floor is divided between additional living quarters and a loft for hay and equipment storage. In addition to the stairway located in the interior passageway, there is a loft-access ramp adjacent to the side entrance (not shown). The building is on a slope (at 3,300′), and there is a retaining wall behind the firewood and storage rooms, creating additional shelter for the passageway. Two cold storage cellars, located under the living room, have outside access only. *a.* main entrance; *b.* warming oven; *c.* wood stove; *d.* privy; *e.* wood storage; *f.* side entrance; *g.* glassed-in porch; *h.* stairs.

Buildings were never painted or stained. The organically minded *Zimmermeister* believed that "protective coatings" don't allow wood to "breathe." It was similarly felt that kiln drying cooks wood, crisping it to death. Buildings were protected by great overhanging gables. Testimony to this method is the age of these wooden structures—commonly 300 to 500 years.

The culmination of alpine architecture can be seen in many magnificent *Bauernhaüser* constructed in Canton Bern during the last century. The vast overhanging gables (often enclosed on the undersides) seem to envelop the structures, sheltering the occupants of an entire farming complex under one fantastic roof—family, stock, tools, hay, provisions.

Interior design was very functional. Almost everything was wood. Hallways were often eliminated, thus saving space and materials. The solid, tongue-and-groove timber walls provided good insulation, and a feeling of privacy and security. Ceilings were kept low to conserve heat and building materials. Doorways had exceptionally large thresholds; these massive timbers being among the structural members holding the completely interlocked *Bauernhäus* together. Another detail, seen in Fig. 163, was a special floorboard, the middle one among adjacent rooms, which extended almost two feet outside the structure. The sides of this floorboard were symetrically tapered leading inwards. When the structural timbers were subjected to thermal expansion, this piece was forced outwards, thus relieving compression forces of the interlocked construction. Many styles of windows were developed, single and double thicknesses. A unique feature was small hinged in-set pane (Fig. 159). Storm shutters were always fitted. There was also a variety of door styles, and a full array of handmade hardware. Sometimes wooden door and gate rails doubled as hinge components. For the animal stalls, double (Dutch) doors were used, letting in light while keeping drafts to a minimum.

In smaller *Alpenhütten*, located high in the alps and used only during the warm summer months, living facilities were kept rudimentary. Eating, sleeping, and Sunday visiting all took place in one room, the *Stübe*. There were one or two rooms for provisions and storage, and perhaps a spare bedroom adjoining the hayloft. The toilet was a privy located at the end of a back porch or sheltered passageway. Often it was positioned directly above the manure tank at the barn.

FIG. 143–Grain loft with rough slate roofing; dated 1651. Canton Ticino. (Courtesy of *Schweizer Bauernhäuser* by Max Gschwend. Bern, Switzerland: Verlag Paul Haupt, 1971.)

FIGS. 144–146–*Bauernhäus* construction of notched timbers. FIG. 145 shows a corner detail. FIG. 146 illustrates how timbers below the gabled roof and balcony are progressively extended to support massive overhangs.

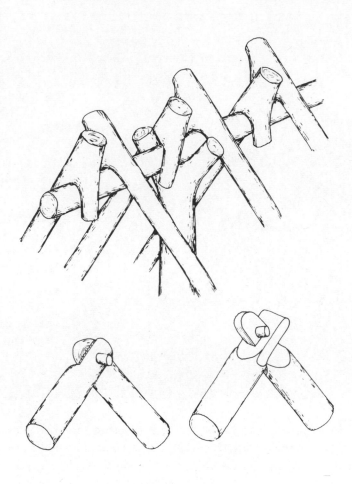

Fig. 147–Methods of securing roofing rafters using pole construction.
Fig. 148–Notching techniques vary in log and timber structures.

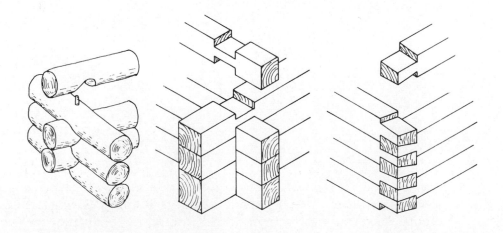

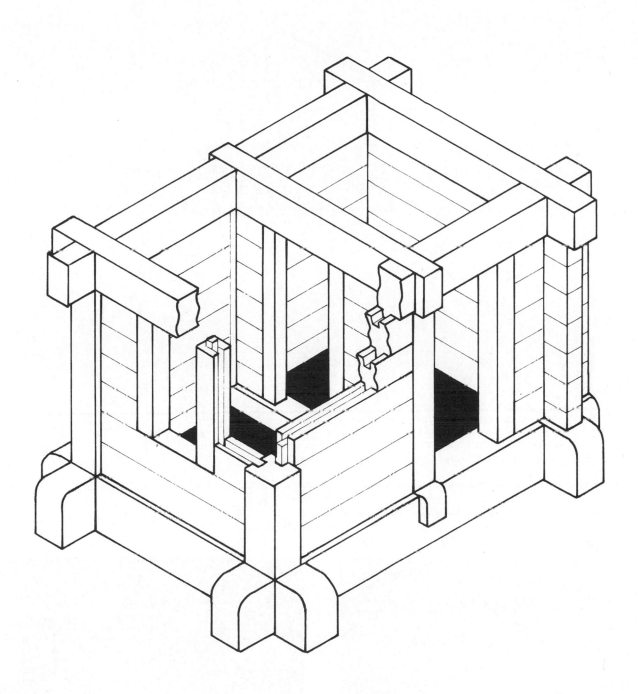

Fig. 149–Isometric diagram of timber construction techniques. Basic concept is creation of a fully interlocked, cubic structure. Base, post, and lintel timbers are fitted by notching. Siding around doors, window, and the interior wall are tongue-and-groove slotted construction. Rear walls continue standard notched "log" technique from the bottom up.

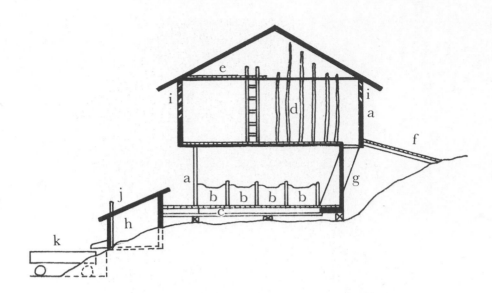

Figs. 150–152–Small barn in Canton Graubünden. Hay is easily transported to the loft via the hillside ramp. Thin poles, seen in Fig. 151, are removable, and serve to keep hay neatly stacked. There is also a gangway, set on the tie beams, for equipment storage. Ventilators, being generous louvers cut through the timber construction, minimize hay spoilage, heat buildup, and chances of spontaneous combustion. Large overhanging gables protect the structure and ensure that the hay remains dry. Hay and feed are dropped downstairs by a built-in shoot. Between the two rows of stalls is a wooden gutter, leading to the manure tank. This tank is emptied by lifting a gate valve fitted above a large spout. A specially built manure wagon may be wheeled directly beneath. Fig. 152 shows how notched timbers are kept in line with vertical doweling which stops warping, a problem when space is left between the logs. *a.* doorway; *b.* stalls; *c.* gutter; *d.* hayloft; *e.* storage; *f.* ramp; *g.* hay shoot; *h.* manure tank; *i.* ventilators; *j.* gate valve; *k.* tank wagon.

Figs. 153, 154–Village barns in a stark and barren valley below Furka Glacier. Long runs of slotted timbers are held in alignment by vertical beams fitted like cotter pins to short horizontal cross-pieces.

FIGS. 155, 156–*Bauernhäus* with cheese-making facilities. An interior control adjusts vent on shingled chimney. Canton Freiburg.

Fig. 157–Riving shingles with froe and maul. Selection of wood is all important. Straight grained pine logs free of knots are cut into 20″ lengths. These pieces are quartered, trimmed of bark, and stored in a ventilated shed to season for one to two years. When work begins, the shingler uses a short broad ax to trim each wedge into a rectangular shape. This is accomplished by cutting out the heartwood and trimming along the sides. These blocks are then split into boards 1″ to 1½″ thick. The next step is done at a bench, well anchored in place before a low, rigid table. Sitting, the shingler places one end of a board on the floor, holding it firmly between knee and table edge. For protection, a heavy leather patch is strapped around his knee. The froe is placed in the center of the board and driven home with a wooden maul. The board is then rived in half with the perpendicular froe handle. Fig. 158 illustrates the progressive stages in riving shingles.

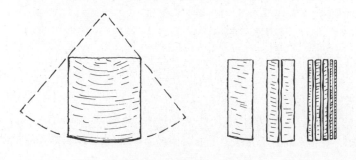

FIG. 159–Fish scale shingles plate an entire house. In addition to storm shutters, windows are double thickness. Half-panes to the right hinge separately. Canton Graubünden.

Fig. 160–Overlapping shingles create insulation during hot and cold
weather. Exposed and weathered shingles protect inner courses,
thus preserving the structure. Canton Freiburg.

FIG. 161–Canton Freiburg.

FIG. 162–Half-timbered framework in-filled with masonry. Canton Bern.

FIG. 163–This enormous *Bauernhaus* was built to accommodate the large farm families of the 18th and 19th centuries. Twelve children were not unusual; and there were often other relatives or hired help in the household. The building also accommodates stock, tools, wagons, sleds, a hay loft, and general storage. Located in a narrow valley at the base of the Alps, the enriched soil fertility and warmer climate made for prosperity invested in a substantial house. Canton Bern.

FIG. 164–*Alpenhütte* interior. Massive threshold under the door is a notched structural cross-member of this *Alpenhütte*. Interior walls are horizontal timbers 5″ thick set into slotted posts. Ceiling is approx. 7′ high. In Swiss woodworking, knots are not frowned upon. In this *Hütte* there is no electricity. A crank telephone is installed. This is not uncommon, as telephones are used for purposes of mountain rescue coordination. Canton Bern.

Fig. 165–*Chirel Alp*–a summer herder's complex. Ninty acres (at 4,600 feet), on the edge of a glacial moraine that once formed a lake bed. The living quarters, built 250–300 years ago, contains cheese making facilities and storage rooms. The upper section contains stalls for stock. A small spare bedroom adjoins the hayloft. Fig. 166–Generally, interlocked construction provides adequate strength; but due to avalanche conditions, a series of massive diagonally braced timbers have been included. These are eight sets of buttresses (*a*) in two rows, four units deep. The stalls are built on several horizontally arranged logs (*b*) set on boulders and bed rock (*c*). Small timbers (*d*) form the center gutters. Removable floor boards (*e*) are notched on the gutter sideboards (*e*), and slope inward for drainage (angle in drawing is exaggerated). Uphill is a stone retaining wall (*f*), backed with rock and shaped to conform with the roof angles. This is to divert avalanches. Picket fence (*g*) keeps stock off the roof.

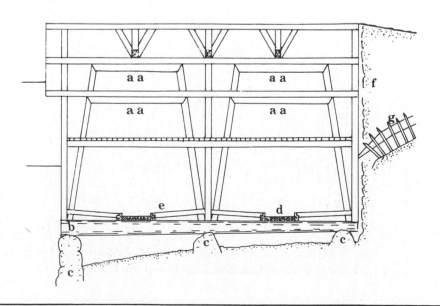

FIG. 167–Truss and diagonal bracing in the hayloft at Chirel Alp. Also seen are the rafters and furring strips to which shingles are nailed. FIG. 168–Diagonal bracing in the stalls. In the lower right is the manure gutter.

FIG. 169–Chirel Alp *Stübe* (eating and sleeping room). FIG. 170–Wooden
knob releases door latch from other side.

FIG. 171–Warming oven. Wonderful to sit on during cold weather. Door for the firebox is in the next room. There is never debris, stuffy air or sucking drafts in the *Stübe*. Heat circulates through partitioned stone chambers, and the stone fire wall. Warmth is gradually radiated throughout the room over many hours. Metal doors with latches on the fire wall (top and right) open to lined boxes for warming food, boots, mittens, etc. Smaller panels and panel on oven front are access for cleaning accumulated soot.

Figs. 172, 173–Small winter barn. Ground level stalls for 2 or 3 cows and
a few calves. The floor is wooden planking. (Hard, cold flooring of
stone or cement may cause joint disease.) Recent additions
include installation of front and rear double doors, and glass
windows. (Living in continual darkness during winter months
weakens cows' eyes.) Canton Bern.

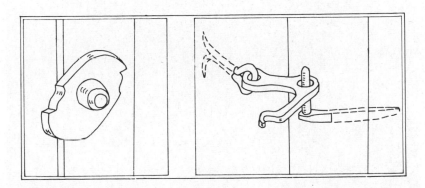

Fig. 174–Left—Spinning wooden door latch. Right—Wrought iron
latch with tangs bent over on the reverse side of panel.
Fig. 175–Handmade wheelbarrow.

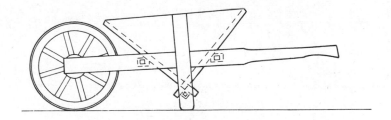

FIG. 176–Cheese being formed and pressed at Chirel Alp. Pressure is released by pulling down on the leather thong attached to a lever which lifts the weighted timber.

XIII. ALPINE DAIRY FARMING

SWITZERLAND is a small, self-contained country where virtually every square yard of land is cherished and used. The geography is that of steep mountains laced with fertile valleys. The most abundant resource is water—there is so much that meadowlands remain moist throughout the warm summer months. Centuries ago the farmers developed methods of working their land for maximum production and minimum destruction. Holdings are generally small, and only a fraction are suitable for intensive row crop agriculture. The people who live in this alpine country are hard workers, extremely conscientious about maintaining their resources. Farmlands have been cultivated for generations, yet few signs of erosion are seen.

As may be expected, most produce and the larger dairy herds are found in the rich valley lands. But the Alps play a functional role, besides serving as an inspiring focus for folk culture. It is customary in Switzerland to send livestock to "summer camp" in the mountains. With their herds out of the way for three or four months, valley farmers are able to concentrate full effort on market crops, grains, and haymaking. The animals are taken to alpine pastures which are usable only during the summer. Sheep and goats graze the higher slopes, which support scanty growth, while cows and their offspring enjoy pastures at middle heights (about 4,500 feet).

Because of their isolation, herders have no practical way of distributing fresh milk to the valley people. Instead, they make cheese, which is kept in storage and sold when they return at the end of summer. In addition to its keeping qualities, cheese making reduces the weight of milk at a ratio of 10:1.

Until recent years the high mountain *Alpenhütten* were accessible only by foot or horse. In early summer a grand parade takes place; when the alpine cheese makers pack their gear and few provisions, and lead the herds into the mountains. For this event the stock is carefully groomed; animals are washed, and favorites garlanded with flowers and giant processional bells. Some bells are cast bronze, others are sheet iron, as large as a yard in circumference. The march into the Alps is colorful, slow, and noisy with the cacophony of clanging bells, mooing and bleating stock, and Alpine yodelling. The farmers, often dressed ceremoniously, walk or ride on a cart. Numerous children help, shouting commands to the herd, and swatting any lagging calves with sticks. This tradition is still carried out by old-timers, and those who live within a few miles of the alpine pastures.

In June the alpine cheese maker (known as a *Senn* in Swiss-German) sets up fencing around the summer pastures. This must be done annually, as winter snows and frequent avalanches destroy fences left standing on steep slopes. Also, pastures can be adjusted to meet the requirements of each season. But what is erected is merely a suggestion of fencing, a sketchy guideline for strong cows and rascally goats. A single strand of barbed wire is commonly used. In the northeastern Alps there is a unique approach using no hardware or fasteners—only crisscrossed stakes and poles stacked in a line (Figs. 93, 94).

We learned about the life and craft of a *Senn* from Armin, who grew up in the Berner-Oberland. Of four brothers and four sisters, three men continue the family tradition.

Mountain life is idyllic as well as rigorous and demanding. The alpine scenery, air, and water are a constant inspiration. A true summer hardly exists. June brings spring weather, but possible snowfalls. July and August are usually warm and sunny, but changeable. Fog is common in the high mountains, as are midsummer hailstorms. First frosts come in August, and snow is expected by September. These weather conditions, plus limitations on hours of direct sunlight made by steep mountain walls, make gardening difficult. But until recently, a *Senn* cut hay and raised his own summer vegetables to supplement a diet of grains and dairy products.

Fig. 177–Pack frame formerly used for portage to a summer *Alpenhütte*.

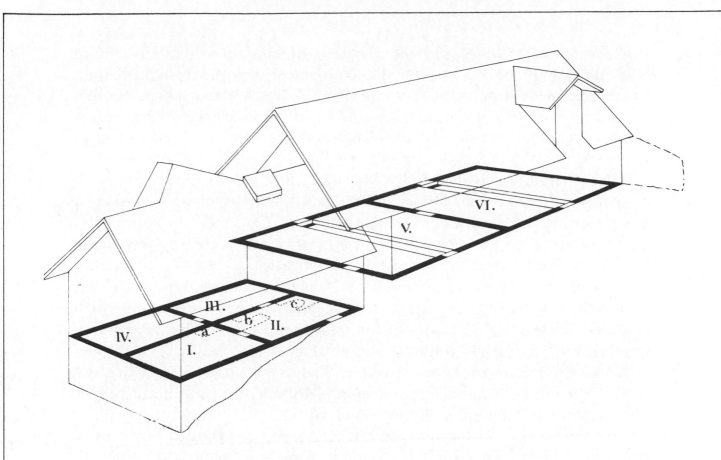

FIG. 178–Chirel Alp. The lower structure serves as living and working quarters. Above and to the rear is the barn, consisting of two rooms, each with a central manure gutter, and a hayloft above. Additional illustrations include FIGS. 165–171, 193. I. *Stübe* (FIG. 172); II. *Küche*; III. spring room; IV. storage; V. & VI. stalls (FIGS. 169–171). *a.* warming oven (FIG. 171); *b.* bake oven-cook stove (FIG. 193); *c.* cheese-making fire pit; *d.* retaining wall.

At an *Alpenhütte*, the central room is the *Küche*, or cheese-making kitchen. The walls and ceiling are black, coated with soot from several hundred years of use. One window lights the room, which is often filled with smoke, creating an atmosphere of mystery and antiquity. The most striking furnishing is the copper cheese-making kettle, which has a capacity of one hundred liters (Fig. 187). Scrubbed daily, the pot shines in contrast to the dark room. This kettle is hung from a massive crane built of timbers 8″ square, and set into pivots in the floor and ceiling. Under the kettle is a fire pit 12″ deep. Enclosing three-fourths of the pit is a low stone wall which functions as a reflector to aid heat distribution. Above is a large, wooden hood to funnel smoke out a narrow slit along the shingled rooftop.

Another prominent feature, seen in Fig. 179, is the great trough carved out of a single tree trunk. Its main function is to drain and collect excess whey as it is pressed from the cheeses. The cheese press (Fig. 176) is located directly above a wide plank set across the trough. Another carved work surface is used as a general table for washing and drying dishes, milk pitchers, cheese forms, and other cheese making utensils. The actual washing takes place in a large, shallow tub placed over the trough. No soap is used, as it would impart a flavor to the milk; wash water is kept hot in a large bucket on top of the stove. A long-handled stainless steel pan serves as a dipper. Fig. 193 depicts the wood-burning stove and bake oven at Chirel Alp.

Behind the *Küche* is a spring room (Fig. 180). This is the creamery. A cold temperature is maintained by the constant flow of water piped in from a spring, then spilling over a large flat rock and onto the stone floor. The room has one exterior wall, with a northeastern exposure, and large ventilating louvers cut into the timbers. Beneath these louvers is another log trough. Here are kept crocks and pitchers of cream, which clabber before the weekly buttermaking. Along a side wall are racks upon which shallow "keelers" of milk are set for cream separation. The large hand-cranked butter churn is also in this room (Fig. 189).

Below the spring room is the cellar. Shelves of aging cheeses line the walls. It is crucial that this room remain dry and cool to obtain proper results. It must also be free of mouse holes.

The *Stübe* is a combination bed and living room. Wooden furniture is plain and scant, often built in. A table, benches and a bed suffice. A warming oven, fed from the *Küche* side of the wall, provides plenty of heat, and a place to dry wet stockings (Fig. 171). Windows look onto views of surrounding mountains.

Fig. 179–Work surface and trough for collecting whey.

FIG. 180–Spring room at Herr Schultz' *Alpenhütte*. Racked on the wall
arc carved skimmers used for separating cream and parting curd,
two milking buckets (with curved staves), and a *Kalberkübel*—used
to feed calves milk and grain.

Each morning we greeted Armin with a handshake, and the local
salutation, *GrüBe* (sounds like "grru-Ssa"). We washed at the outdoor
water trough (Fig. 181), then helped with chores until breakfast at 7:00.
This meal was always a treat (see Chap. XIV).

Milking time followed. In the Alps during the summer, the cows graze
at night, returning to the barns during the day to chew their cud. We were
told this protects them from large biting flies that breed during warm
weather. Usually the cows return on their own, shortly after sunrise. But
sometimes they continue to graze. In this case, the *Senn* goes after them. On
most days only the milking cows need be brought back. Calves and heifers
generally graze a different pasture, and return on their own during
milking time. Occasionally, a young calf wanders off and gets lost. Then
someone must go after it.

Altogether, Armin kept 9 milking cows, 6 heifers, 10 calves, and 4 goats
at Chirel Alp through most of the summer. Only two milkers were his, the
remaining stock belonging to other farmers. In midsummer the barn was
full; and by early autumn, the four small pastures had been grazed quite
low.

In the barn, each animal is tethered at a regular place along a rail, facing the wall. Down the center is a gutter, about 3″ wide and 6″ deep. During the day this gutter fills with manure, which is periodically shoveled to one end. For cleanup, a trap block is lifted to reveal a slot in front of the door, and the accumulation is pushed through into a large tank below.

In Switzerland it is the custom to tie up the tails of the milking cows in the barn. This is done to keep their tails raised off the gutter floor, as well as preventing an obstinate cow from swishing a milker in the face. The tails are tied to a simple device—a light cable strung beneath the ceiling, directly above the ledge of the manure gutter. One end is fastened to the front wall; the other passes through a hole in the back wall, and is tied to a heavy rock. From this cable are tied lengths of stout twine, approx. 3′ long, to which the tails are tied with a slip knot. When a cow reclines, the cable slackens to accommodate the downward pull. After their tails are tied, each cow is given a handful of salt, which she accepts most enthusiastically—almost drowning the offered hand. At their stanchions (which at Chirel Alp have been nailed securely to serve as a manger) the stock is sometimes given hay, but never grains. These healthy animals live on grass after they are one year old. They are not given water in the barn. We were told that water increases quantity, not quality, of milk. In pasture, however, there is always access to a stream or spring-fed trough.

FIG. 181–Water trough at Chirel Alp.

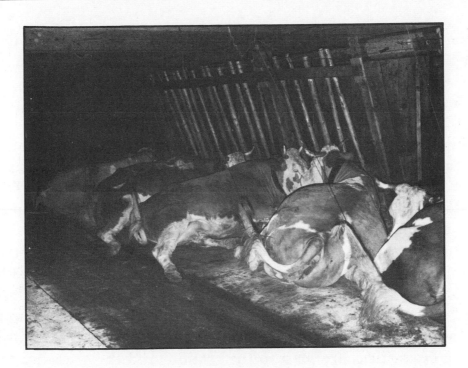

Fig. 182–Milk cows chewing their cud. Cows' tails are tied to an overhead cable.

Each morning is occupied by milking and cheese making. Afternoon tasks vary—from building repairs and gardening, to spreading manure and hauling wood. A major task for dairy farmers is cutting, drying, and storing hay for winter feed. If hay must be purchased it becomes impossible to earn a living. Armin must provide for his two cows through the winter months, besides keeping a supply at Chirel Alp in case of summer storms. Part of the hay comes from the valley farms, but the higher meadows are cut as well.

It is only within recent years that any machinery has been developed for cutting hay on steep inclines. Even now, a scythe is used by the traditional *Senn*, and those working the steepest slopes. Hay has been cut on these mountainsides for generations, yet we seldom saw signs of erosion. One explanation is that abundant ground water keeps grasses growing continually, resulting in a strong and complex root system within the soil. The grass must be cut annually; if allowed to grow too long, snow will get stuck in it, and the weight will pull clumps of sod out of the hillside. Steep slopes that have been cleared of rocks and stumps for hay growing are not used for grazing. The hay itself is a mixture of wild grasses that flower at different times throughout the summer.

Reaping in the Alps is a refined labor. The scythe is extremely light, seeming weightless for such a large implement. With minimal inertia to overcome, its use is an easy swinging motion. The action is such that the blade slices the hay, rather than cutting against it. This technique requires many swings, but it can be almost effortless. Legs are held slightly apart, knees bent, and the whole body rotates in rhythm with the tool as it drifts along just above the ground.

The blade is kept razor sharp. A whetstone for this purpose is always carried in a *Stienfas* (a carved wooden sheath), which is filled with water and hung from the belt while working. Every so often the *Senn* pauses for a few moments, and the scythe is expertly sharpened. The blade is also kept very thin. Wear caused by repeated sharpening exposes a thicker section of metal. Periodically the edge must be pounded thin. This is done with a hammer and stake made for the purpose.

After harvest, the hay is dried. Weather plays a crucial role. Often hay is left on the ground a few days, then flipped over using a light, wooden fork (Fig. 184). This method is slow and risks mildew. To avoid spoilage, different devices are used to stack green hay for maximum air circulation and exposure. These usually follow regional conventions. In some places, poles with cross sticks are set into the ground, and the grass draped over. Bernese farmers prefer a hinged tripod, somewhat like an artist's easel. We also saw a clothesline-like affair constructed of stakes and wire.

Fig. 183–Armin milking. The Alpine milking stool, with wooden seat and one middle leg. An attached leather belt buckles around the *Senn.*

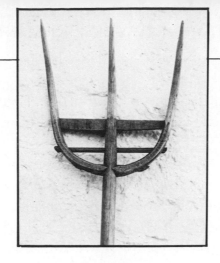

FIG. 184–Hay fork.

When the hay is dry, it is much lighter in weight, and can be swept into piles with a light, wooden rake. The hay is then put in storage. This is either in haystacks, which are carefully built to shed rain and remain dry on the inside; or into a hayloft, more convenient for winter use.

Moving hay from mountainside to barn is done with a net, and the opposite corners are tied together with the aid of wooden blocks called *Holtztrügeln* (Fig. 185). If the way is clear below, the whole bundle is set free to roll. Otherwise, it must be carried over the shoulders, and the weight may approach two hundred pounds.

Land maintenance is crucial in any viable agriculture. For the *Senn*, care-taking involves several operations. Already mentioned are the strictly followed timbering practices and haying on the steeper slopes. Land is also continually cleared of deadwood and large rocks, and fertilized with manure.

Cow manure (*mist*) is recycled as completely as possible. Eighty percent of the manurial constituents in the food of a milk cow is voided. Her annual excrement, per 1000 lbs. live weight, amounts to some 28,000 lbs., of which 19,000 lbs. are solid and 8,000 lbs. are liquid. Manure is a perishable substance. Losses up to 50 percent of the potential value can easily result from leaching, scattering, and evaporation. Urine generally contains more nitrogen and potassium than solid dung. Enzymes and other digestive juices at work in manure stimulate development of beneficial bacteria and natural antibiotics in the soil. At Chirel Alp a concrete manure tank is built into the hillside directly below the rear entrance to the barn:

"In the enclosed pit, the manure soon becomes impregnated and completely enclosed by an atmosphere of carbon dioxide having also a relatively high humidity. Under these conditions, manure breaks down semi-anaerobically to form a product that is unusually high in the important nutrient elements. *There seem to be very little or no losses of nitrogen or other elements when manures are fermented in a properly constructed enclosed pit.*"[*]

---

[*] J. I. Rodale, *Encyclopedia of Organic Gardening*. Rodale Books, Inc., 1971.

This pit is constructed so that a wagon fitted with a wooden container can be pulled below the tank and filled with the soupy contents. A similar arrangement is seen in Fig. 150. In past years, these wagons were pulled by horse, and in some instances, expecially at farms without road access, this is still the practice. The *mistwagon* is driven back and forth, throughout the different pastures. Built in is a wide sliding gate valve that emits a continuous dribble of liquid manure. Where the vehicle cannot negotiate, the *Senn* stops to spread manure using a bucket attached to a pole. On the steepest slopes it is necessary to carry manure on one's back. A wooden tank-pack is made for this purpose. The principle recognized by alpine dairymen is the necessity of constantly putting back into the soil as much as possible. It is through this effort that the Alps afford a means of livelihood year after year.

Pastureland must be not only constantly enriched, but also cleared of winter's debris—deadwood and rock brought down the mountainside by avalanches. If allowed to accumulate, debris takes up valuable space where grass cannot grow or cows graze. Large pieces of wood or rock can damage the sod if left to be dragged down by the next year's snow. Debris is gathered into piles where the deadwood is burned.

In early spring, when the ground is covered with well-packed snow, trees are felled for the next winter's use. Logs are hauled from the woodlot and cut into exact one meter lengths. They are then stacked to season through the warmer months. At the end of summer some logs are bucked into thirds, then split with a heavy wedging maul. These are stored for next summer's use. The other logs are transported to the valley farm.

Fig. 185–*Holtztrügeln*. Wooden device used for many tying needs on the alpine dairy farm. Small blocks (3″) are made for tying adjustable cheese forms. Large ones (up to 12″) are used while hauling logs. These are very helpful as they are especially easy to fasten, adjust, or loosen. In use, a simple loop is inserted through the central hole and around the projecting horn. The only care is that the leading end crosses under the incoming length. Also, the rope diameter must be large enough to fit snugly in the carved channels.

FIG. 186–Cream skimmers.

SCHWEIZER ALPKÄSE   Swiss Alpine Cheese

This is a hard, slightly salty, yellow cheese, aged at least eight months, but usually eaten after one year. Placed vertically on a shelf in a cool, dry cellar, it will keep for thirty years. The size of a round varies between ten and twenty pounds. The term *Alpkäse* is a description of an approach to cheese making, rather than being a specific cheese. With years of experience, each *Senn* develops his own variations of the technique. There are few controls available in the mountains. Cows' milk fluctuates in quality and flavor throughout the summer as different grasses bloom in pastures undergoing continual change. Conditions in one cheese cellar as compared to another are different, and none remains stable from month to month.

These variations, combined with a relatively small production, make it impractical to market *Alpkäse* through commercial channels. Previously, each village sent its herds to the alpine pastures with a local *Senn*, and cheese was distributed to the farmers at the end of the summer as part of the transaction. Now, each cheese maker has a wider clientele, developed over many seasons. Local and city people find their way to his door, sample the wares of his cellar, and purchase their favorite mountain-made cheeses.

50 to 80 quarts fresh milk*	2 cheesecloths (described on pg. 166)
giant cauldron	cheese hoop, or form
submersible thermometer	1″ thick board (slightly larger than
cream skimmer, or paddle	the cheese form)
cheese harp, or whisk	press, or weight
¼ cup salt	dry, cool cellar
rennet†	

---

* Use no less than 20 quarts. With small cheeses the difficulty is curing, as the surface area is comparatively great, causing the cheese to dry rather than age.

† Armin uses a crystaline rennet powder manufactured by Chr. Hansen in Denmark

In a copper cauldron, very slowly heat milk. Half may be skimmed milk (but not nonfat). At 90° remove the pot from direct heat. While the milk heats, set ⅓ tsp. powdered rennet preparation onto the surface of 1 cup cold water to which a small handful of salt has been added. Allow this to stand undisturbed. After 15 to 20 minutes, add 1 quart warm milk to the rennet. Using two pitchers, pour the mixture back and forth several times to blend thoroughly. Pour into the kettle and stir vigorously for 15 seconds. Cover and allow to stand.

In 15 to 30 minutes, a soft, delicate, white rennet custard should form. Gently divide custard with a creamskimmer (Fig. 186), or similar utensil. Continue parting this floating mass with slow, careful strokes for 2 to 3 minutes. Next a whisk is needed. This may be the traditional variety, made of a small pine tree, a stainless steel cheese harp (Fig. 187), or a large kitchen whisk. Carefully continue to separate the custard into smaller fragments, which become curd floating in whey. Curd is heavy and sinks to the bottom if whisking is discontinued. Stirring should be in a D-motion, so as not to create a whirlpool, or allow the curd to gather into a single lump. After whisking 20 to 30 minutes, check the temperature, and very slowly rewarm to 90°. Continue whisking for a total of 50 to 60 minutes. Stop when the curd is small, rather spongy, sweet to taste and slightly squeaky when chewed. Stir curd into a small whirlpool and allow it to settle. This will center the curd into a mass on the bottom of the cauldron. Reach into the pot, and carefully press curd together.

Next remove curd from whey using a heavy cheesecloth, three feet square, made of coarsely woven linen. An assistant's hand is helpful. Take two corners of the cloth, and

Fig. 187–Herr Schultz cutting curd with a stainless steel cheese harp.

FIG. 188–Fitting curd into an adjustable cheese hoop. Whey is seen draining into the trough below.

carefully slip it under the curd. Gather the four corners together, and remove from the cauldron. Place cloth and curd into a large hoop or cheese form set on a drainboard. Open the cloth. Push the mass of curd down into the mold, using fists (Fig. 188). Fold corners of the cloth over the curd. Adjust the hoop so that the curd is approximately 1 inch above the hoop rim. (If a mold is used, the correct size is somewhat smaller than the volume of curd. Also, there must be drainage holes in the bottom.) Place a board on top of the folded cloth. After 20 to 30 minutes, remove board and hoop. Fold back the cloth and trim off excess cheese. Place a clean cloth over the cheese. Refit hoop and turn over. Remove the first cheesecloth (now on top) to a tub of cold rinse water. Fold corners of the fresh cloth over the cheese and replace board. In 1 hour repeat trimming and turning process. Use a clean replacement cloth. Next apply the press for one-half hour. Then turn cheese over and refit the press. Continue this half-hour cycle—trimming, changing the cloth, and turning—for 3 to 4 hours. Then extend to every 2 hours for 6 hours.

Next morning remove hoop and take cheese to the cellar for curing. Immerse in a salt-water bath for 24 hours. Dry cheese, and place flat on a shelf for two months. During this period turn once daily, sprinkle with a little salt, and rub with a wet cloth to form the rind. Cellar temperature should be maintained at 40° to 45° during the aging time— at least six more months.

ZIEGENKÄSE   Alpine Goat Cheese

Next to mountain spring water, goat milk is the essence of alpine purity. Goats are more selective than cows; they browse rather than graze. Goats climb to higher pastures, thus always eating the freshest herbs, which remain in a stage of springtime tenderness throughout summer. Because goats give less milk (and few farmers keep large herds), goat cheeses are made in small sizes—approximately two pounds. *Ziegenkäse* is soft and white, and sometimes smelly.

Place a pail of 8 to 10 quarts of goats' milk into a large pan of water on top of the stove. Heat to 85°. Remove water pan and milk from fire. Dissolve rennet in ½ cup lukewarm water. Stir rennet thoroughly into milk. Let stand 30 to 40 minutes. Begin to stir carefully with a wire whisk, breaking up the custard which has formed. After curd and whey begin to separate, reheat very slowly for 10 minutes. Stir continuously. Allow a maximum temperature of 85°. Remove milk pail from water, and allow curd to settle 5 minutes. Pour off half the whey. With hands, gather curd into a mass. Lift out curd and place in a cheese form* lined with cheesecloth. Lightly pat curd into form. Fold excess cloth over cheese and place a small weight (such as a heavy pot lid) on top. After 5 or 10 minutes turn over. Turn cheese every half-hour for 2 to 3 hours. Then lengthen cycle to every 2 hours until bedtime.

In the morning the cheese is ready for curing. Place in a salt-water bath for 24 hours. Turn and rub with salt once daily for one month. *Ziegenkäse* is ripe and ready to eat in six to eight weeks.

FIG. 189 – Butter churn mounted on curved pine roots. Inside the churn is a slot carved through the hub. Into this is fitted the butter paddle, a flat pine board, with four 1″ holes bored through each end. The churn is filled less than half full with clabbered cream. As the paddle turns, it passes through the cream, which stays on the bottom.

---

* The traditional form is made of pine, with four short legs and a lid to place on top of the cheese. The important thing is correct size for a snug fit, and drainage holes in the bottom.

FIG. 190–Kneading fresh butter at Chirel Alp.

BUTTER

At Chirel Alp butter making is a weekly joy beginning before sunrise on Sunday. Cream from each morning's milking goes into the cheese kettle, but evening milk is poured into wide, shallow tubs kept in the spring room. Overnight, cream rises to the top in a thick layer. With a wooden skimmer, such as those shown in Fig. 186, it is easy to transfer the cream into a ceramic crock where it will clabber before butter making. Crocks are submerged in a water trough if the weather is too warm.

FIG. 191–Churn detail.

FIG. 192.

ALPINE ECONOMICS

Monetary returns for cheese making are minimal relative to the labor involved and the economic situation of modern Switzerland. A large percentage of herders—those interested in making money—board only non-milking stock, and no longer make cheese. (Only those who return to the Alps each summer out of love are the cheese makers.)

It is figured that one cow eats daily a measure of hay equivalent in value to 8 liters milk. One liter (wholesale) is worth 50 *Rappen*, or one-half a Swiss Frank (in 1972 about 26 cents). The daily milk production for an average mountain cow is:

June   12   liters per day
July   11.5 liters per day
August   10   liters per day
September   10   liters per day

3 calves (0–1 years old) = 1 cow, or 4 Frank per day
3 calves (1–2 years old) = 2 cows, or 8 Frank per day
1 heifer (2–3 years old) = 1 cow, or 4 Frank per day
8 goats (adult) = 1 cow

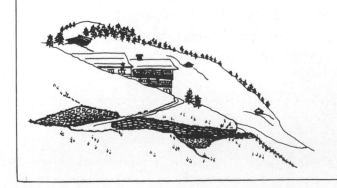

FIG. 193–Bake oven and cook stove at Chirel Alp.

XIV. ALPINE CUISINE

ALPINE cuisine is simple and sturdy fare—basically milk and cheese, bread and potatoes—graced with a few delicacies such as sweet butter, fresh cream, and wild berries from mountain woods and meadows. Many *Alpenhütten* are above timberline, and all are restricted as far as gardening is concerned by an extremely short growing season and unreliable alpine weather. Lower down, the weather is more accomodating; and although the risk of summer frosts and hailstorms remains, bountiful gardens are tucked close beside every farmhouse. Formerly, when no automobile roads reached the summer *Alp*, herders were more dependent on what they could grow, as all provisions had to be packed by horse or on one's back. Now, an occasional trip to the family farm down in the valley can be made to replenish supplies.

The kitchen at an *Alpenhütte* doubles as a cheese making room, and cooking facilities are relatively primitive. Most of the cooking is done in pots on top of the wood-burning stove; boiled potatoes, soups, stews, and porridge are often on the menu. Large bread bakings are done in a wood-fired oven.

Often there is little time for cooking. For our favorite and most frequent meal, the table held a pitcher of milk (from the favorite cow), a loaf of dark, homemade wheat bread, and several types of cheese.

CHEESE

The infinite variety and unfailing presence at mealtimes of cheese are clear indications of the special place this food has in the hearts and stomachs of the Swiss. The cheese of each canton, district, and even each *Alp* is unique. The pale yellow, large-holed type called "Swiss Cheese" is actually the specialty of the Emmental district of Canton Bern, a fertile valley able to support large dairy herds. *Emmentalerkäse* is made in huge thousand liter copper vats, and the finished cheese may weigh 200 pounds. *Gruyère* cheese is another famous Swiss export used in many recipes. Cheese sampling at an *Alpenhütte* is an adventure, as the products are variable and available only on the very mountains on which they are made. These cheeses include *Ziger* (soft fresh cheese), *Ziegenkäse* (creamy goat cheese), *Alpkäse* (hard alpine cheese), smoked *Ziger*, and other varieties. Recipes for making *Alpkäse* and *Ziegenkäse* are given in Chapter XIII.

ARMIN'S ALPINE *MUESLI*

This cereal was our morning meal at Chirel Alp—a generous bowl of seeds, nuts and wild berries covered with sweet cream and a sprinkling of grains. Heavenly food, and quite sustaining.

½ cup flax seeds	oat, rye, or wheat flakes
1½ cups warm water	walnuts, hazelnuts, or almonds, chopped
¼ cup dried currants or raisins	1 or more cups fresh berries
2 to 6 Tbs. wheat germ	cream

Soak flax seeds and raisins (or currants) in warm water overnight. In the morning, mash berries to release juice, and blend into seeds. Add wheat germ and chopped nuts. Sprinkle on flaked grain. Stir in cream or top milk to desired consistency. We used what was available: raspberries, blueberries, strawberries, or sometimes other fresh fruit; sunflower seeds, pine nuts, dates; fresh, soft *Ziger* (try sieved cottage cheese in place of *Ziger*). Proportions changed according to what was on hand, and how many berries we found. Cultured milk or yogurt is a delicious substitute for cream or milk.

MUESLI II

A summer evening meal. Serves six.

assorted fresh fruit: apples, pears, apricots, banana, berries . . .	¼ cup wheat germ
1 Tbs. lemon juice	¼ cup sunflower seeds
3 Tbs. honey	½ cup raw oat flakes
½ cup nutmeats	6 to 12 pitted dates, chopped
	1 quart yogurt

Grind nuts, seeds and oats (toast slightly, if desired) in a food mill to make coarse meal. Mix in wheat germ and chopped dates. Cut fruit into bite-size pieces. Thin honey with lemon juice to make syrup. Pour over fruit. Mix dry ingredients with fruit. Gently blend in yogurt.

APRICOT DELIGHT

One of the luxuries of alpine living is the unlimited supply of sweet fresh cream to whip, sour, pour over berries, or drink plain. Use enough of each ingredient to delight you and your friends.

dried apricots	pine nuts, if available
wheat germ	whipping cream
cashews, or hazelnuts, ground fine.	

Line the bottom of a deep-sided baking dish with dried apricots. Cover with boiling water, and allow the fruit to stand overnight, or until it has softened and absorbed most of the liquid. Amount of water added should be slightly more than apricots absorb. In the morning, sprinkle on wheat germ, pine nuts, and whatever. Cover with whipped cream. Serve.

SOUR CREAM

To 1 cup heavy cream add 1 tsp. lemon juice or vinegar, or 2 tsp. sour milk (must be unpasteurized). Let stand until thick. Or, allow unpasteurized cream to sour naturally in a cool place (if left in a warm place it will separate—another process, used to make cream cheese). Natural souring may take several days.

CULTURED MILK

Allow whole, unpasteurized cows' or goats' milk to stand in a warm place (85°–95°) overnight, or until milk thickens. Drink plain, with berries, or otherwise flavored.

OAT PORRIDGE

½ cup steel-cut oats	pinch of salt
2½ cups milk	handful of raisins

Cook ingredients in a double boiler (or in a saucepan set in a larger pan of water). Allow 45 minutes. Serve with fresh berries and fruit-honey syrup.

MITTAGESSEN

Noon dinner is the main meal of the day, designed to refuel a hard-working farm family and sustain them through a long afternoon of vigorous activity. Hearty soup, potato, and grain dishes are common, supplemented generously with fresh garden vegetables and fruits in season. Bread and cheese are always on the menu, kept handy in a drawer under the dining table.

CREAM of NETTLES

Gather one large bucketful of nettle greens—tops and first sets of leaves from young, tender plants. Wear gloves to avoid stings. Wash greens by stirring in water with a long-handled spoon. Pour this water off, then pour one quart or more boiling water into the bucket with the greens and cover as if brewing tea. Let stand a few minutes; nettles will lose their stinging properties. Drain in a colander, saving the juice in another pot. Chop greens fine with knife or kitchen shears. Melt a good amount of butter (4 Tbs.) in a large deep skillet. Sauté a chopped onion and minced garlic clove. Add nettles. Stir in ½ to 1 cup cracked or bulgar wheat. Add reserved nettle "tea" gradually as needed. Cover with a lid and stir occasionally until wheat is soft. Add salt to taste. Remove from fire and stir in 2 to 3 tablespoons cream or sour cream. Serve with hot baked potatoes.

GERSTENSUPPE   Barley Soup

½ to 1 cup whole barley	1 cup leeks, chopped
8 cups water or stock	1 cup celery with leaves, chopped
1 tsp. salt	4 Tbs. butter
1 onion, chopped	½ cup cream
1 bay leaf	freshly ground black pepper
1 or 2 tomatoes	handful of parsley, chopped
2 carrots, sliced	

In the soup pot gently sauté onion in 2 Tbs. butter. Add water or stock, barley and bay leaf (bouillon is optional). Cook 1 hour. Add salt and vegetables (except parsley), simmer until tender. Before serving add butter and cream. Stir to blend. Garnish with black pepper and parsley.

CRACKED WHEAT and VEGETABLES

1 cup cracked wheat	1½ to 2 quarts water or whey
½ cup diced potato	1 tsp. salt
2 leeks	parsley and chives
1 carrot	2 to 3 Tbs. butter
1 or 2 cloves garlic	

Melt butter in a large iron skillet. Sauté chopped leeks, carrot, potato, and garlic. Add wheat, stirring to brown evenly. Remove wheat and vegetables to a pot of boiling water or whey. Simmer, stirring occasionally, until tender, about 45 minutes. Remove from fire, and garnish with a handful of chopped parsley and chives before serving.

RACLETTE

Raclette is traditionally prepared by exposing a section of cheese to an open fire, then scraping the melted portion onto a heated plate. Small boiled new potatoes are added to the plate, accompanied by dill pickles and pickled onions.

1 to 2 lbs. *Raclette* cheese	**pickles and onions**
8 to 12 boiled new potatoes	**mustard and horseradish**

Preheat 4 oven-proof plates at 450° for 5 minutes. At an open fireplace, expose an edge of the cheese to the heat. Allow the surface to melt, then quickly scrape it off with a knife onto the hot plates. Serve with hot potatoes, pickles and onions. Pass mustard and horseradish. Prepare two or three servings of *raclette* for each person.

Raclette may also be prepared in an oven. Cut cheese into slices ⅛ inch thick, 5 inches long and 2 inches wide. Remove hot plates from oven and arrange a fan of cheese slices in the center of each plate. Place plates on a rack close to the floor of the oven. Cheese will melt in about 1 minute; do not allow it to brown, even slightly. Remove plates from oven, place potatoes and condiments on the side, and serve immediately.

RÖSTI

Shredded potatoes fried into a crusty, golden cake.

6 to 8 baking potatoes	**4 Tbs. butter**
½ cup chopped onion	**2 Tbs. oil**
½ tsp. salt	

Drop potatoes in enough boiling water to cover and cook for 10 minutes. Drain and cool 1 hour. Sauté onions in butter. Just before frying, grate potatoes into long strips and toss lightly with salt and onions. Heat oil and butter in a heavy 10 inch skillet until sputtering. Spread potatoes evenly in the pan, packing them down with a spatula. Fry uncovered for 8 to 10 minutes. When underside is brown and crusty, place a plate upside-down over the potatoes. Hold skillet and plate firmly together, and invert. If necessary add a few tablespoons butter to the skillet. Then slide the potato cake back into the skillet to brown the second side. Fry 6 to 8 minutes.

POTATOES AND RHUBARB

A midday meal: boiled new potatoes, rhubarb sauce, and whipped cream. Place a pile of tiny boiled garden potatoes in the middle of the table, then a bowl of rhubarb and another of whipped cream. Each person chops up some potatoes on his plate, covers them with rhubarb sauce, and tops it with a dollop of cream. A cup of hot coffee-milk is always served with this meal.

Rhubarb Sauce:	**¼ cup water**
4 cups rhubarb stalks, chopped	**¾ cup honey or sugar**

Steam rhubarb in water in a tightly covered saucepan. Cook 15 to 20 minutes, until rhubarb is soft, but not broken. Stir in sweetening over low heat until thoroughly dissolved.

FRUIT PIE

A meal to make an old man's eyes pop (which they very nearly did) is fresh fruit pie served as a main course. *GroBmutter* (Grandmother) sets this open-faced pie on the table fresh from the oven and full of sun-ripened flavor.

Pastry crust for 1 large pie, or 2 or 3 smaller pies:

3 cups fine flour	1 tsp. vanilla extract
6 Tbs. sugar	3 Tbs. lemon juice
½ tsp. salt	1 cup plus 2 Tbs. softened butter
3 egg yolks	

Combine dry ingredients. Add and work in egg yolks, vanilla, and lemon juice. Work in butter. Make a ball when mixture is no longer sticky. Cover and chill one half-hour. Roll to ⅛ inch thickness. Line baking pan(s) with dough.

Filling:
6 to 8 cups fruit (apricots, peaches, apples, plums, cherries, berries, etc.)
2 to 3 Tbs. lemon juice, if fruit is very sweet
4 Tbs. sugar or honey, if fruit is not sweet enough

Wash, core or pit, and slice fruit, as necessary. Arrange fruit in rows over crust. Make one or more layers. Squeeze on lemon juice, or sprinkle on sugar or honey. Bake in preheated oven at 400° for 7 to 10 minutes. Reduce the heat to 350° and continue to bake 10 to 30 minutes, depending on softness of fruit.

Variations: 1. Cover pie crust with ¼ inch layer of finely ground nutmeats, applesauce, or tart jam. Layer fruit on top. 2. Make a custard of 2 or 3 egg yolks beaten with ½ cup cream and ½ cup sugar or honey. Pour over fruit after first 10 minutes of baking. Or, cook custard in top of double boiler, and pour over pie when both have cooled. 3. Bake pie crust in oven for 7 to 10 minutes without filling. Fill with fresh fruit when cooled. Top with whipped cream.

SOUP TO EAT BEFORE PIE

1 quart onion soup	1 cup grated *Gruyère* cheese
1 cup bread cubes, dry	chopped parsley

Prepare onion soup. Add bread cubes and stir in grated cheese. Allow cheese to melt. Garnish with parsley.

BOILED NEW POTATOES

Combined with a platter of cheeses and a leafy green salad, boiled potatoes (especially garden fresh new potatoes) are a delicious and traditional Swiss meal.

Prepare 3 to 5 new potatoes for each serving. Wash and drop in boiling water to cover. Cook potatoes, covered, until tender. Melt 3 to 6 Tbs. butter in a skillet. Add potatoes and roll them about gently over low heat until they are well coated. Garnish with fresh parsley, chives, or dill, chopped fine. Season with salt and serve with horseradish.

DINNER

The evening meal in Switzerland is customarily light. Often it is similar to the morning meal of bread and cheese, with hot tea or coffee. Sometimes potatoes or a fruit or vegetable is added. At Chirel Alp we ate supper at about 7:00—after milking and barn chores—and we were ready to sleep soon afterward.

SUNDAY AT ARMIN'S

A most memorable evening meal on a summery Sunday at Chirel Alp: fruit salad and cream soup . . . one bowl ripe apricots, peaches, strawberries, blueberries, and raspberries . . . one bowl sweet, cool cream.

BAKING DAY

In the days of Armin's father, farmers in the mountain valley below Chirel Alp kept goats and pigs, and grew fields of wheat, barley, rye, and oats. They milled their grains, and from that flour baked bread. Today a switch has been made from goats to cows, which produce more milk and meat, and are more profitable in a cash economy. Most farmers raise hay to feed their animals, but they buy bread from the baker.

Armin prefers to bake bread in his own style. He grinds wheat with a hand mill, and adds only whey left over from cheese making—no leavening. Baked in a stone oven, the loaves are thick-crusted, dark and heavy. This bread stores well, and is made in quantities that provide a 6 to 8 week supply. Each loaf weighs over 2 pounds. The crust is thick and crunchy, but inside it is soft and moist. This bread is chewed slowly and thoroughly, which allows more time to enjoy its full wheaty flavor. The taste is deeply satisfying, and even more wonderful with sweet butter.

One loaf: | **1 cup cracked wheat meal**
6 cups coarsely ground flour | **3½ cups hot whey (or water and 1 Tbs. salt)**

Soak cracked wheat in hot whey several hours, or overnight. Add flour to make a stiff dough. Knead 300 times. Shape into loaf and place in a greased pan. Cover with a damp towel and let sit 12 to 24 hours in a warm place. Bake at 350° for 1½ hours.

If using a wood-burning stove, preheat the oven 30 to 60 minutes. Bake the bread in 2 smaller loaves for approximately 2 hours. Try to keep the heat uniform. Rotate loaves if baking is uneven.

xv. *DER SCHWEIZER KÜFER**

THE SWISS COOPER

THROUGHOUT our travels we saw how close to the vanishing edge of existence were the crafts and craftsmen that we wished to learn from. We felt disillusioned regarding our dreams of their survival in Europe, and so were constantly reminded of the urgency to find those remaining teachers. We gradually realized that our home was America, and so wished to instill the essence of this journey deep into our beings before returning.

An apprenticeship came as the answer. We thought about the alpine traditions carefully preserved in the mountains of Switzerland and decided to stay in the Berner-Oberland. We knew that we could live with Armin at Chirel Alp; we would approach Herr Kohler, a *Küfermeister* (alpine bucket maker), with the idea of taking on a student.

Upon our arrival, Herr Kohler took me into the workshop almost immediately to introduce his craft. The *Küfer* is most similar to the "white cooper" of old rural England—a kind of dairyman's bucket maker. Herr

FIG. 194–Milking buckets.

* By Drew.

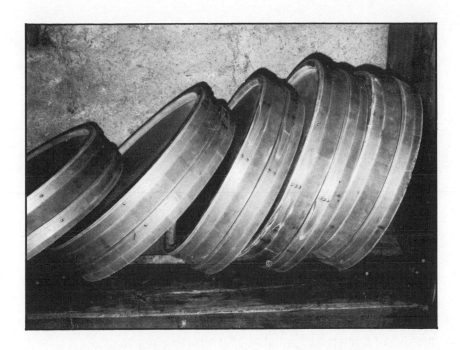

FIG. 195–"Keelers"—cream separation tubs.

Kohler took his apprenticeship exactly 50 years before I came to him. Only since 1967 has he devoted full time to woodworking. Previously, as is customary with his craft, he spent each summer as a *Senn* (alpine cheese maker and herder) and had his own barn full of animals. He had time for woodcraft in winter only.

The *Küfer* makes a variety of articles used at an *Alpenhütte*. These include milking buckets, feeding buckets, butter churns, creamery tubs, and washtubs for dairy and household use. However, as with other craftsmen, the rise of industrialization has led to the demise of this handcraft. A great deal of skill and labor is involved in making his wares; e.g., at least ten hours of intense work by a master craftsman yields one milking bucket, which then commonly gives fifty or even one hundred years' use. In modern Switzerland a *Küfer* must ask a relatively high price for such an item, and a farmer inheriting his father's *Alp* needs to purchase little new equipment. The alpine dairymen are becoming fewer in number and valley farmers are prohibited by law from using wooden vessels and utensils. In 1972 Herr Kohler knew of only nine coopers working in Switzerland.

The process and technique that I began to learn involved a variety of skills. I do not purport to give full instructions for becoming a *Küfer*. Rather, I wish to recount experiences as an apprentice, and transmit an idea of what is involved in such a sophisticated country craft.

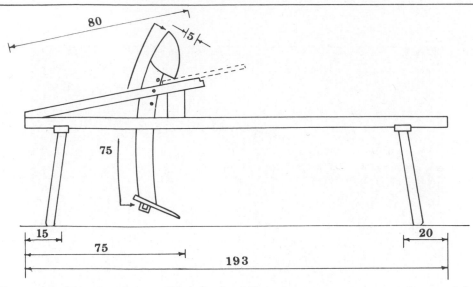

FIG. 196–Shaving horse. The dashed line represents a stave clamped in place. (Dimensions in centimeters.)

MAKING A *KÜBEL* (wooden bucket)

As the first step in *Kübelmachen* (bucket making), Herr Kohler showed me a two-man crosscut saw and a long-handled ax. To be a *Küfer* one must first be an accomplished woodsman. The process begins with selection and felling of the finest pine trees. After stripping, the trunk is cut into 20″ lengths (ill. *a*). These are split into pie-shaped wedges for drying (ill. *b*). Seasoning requires at least two years; five years or more is preferred. If the wood is not aged the finished *Kübel* will shrink, and no longer retain liquids. While aging, the wood looks like particularly fine cord wood, cut and wedged for the fireplace. The wood must have straight, even grain. Tiny knots make work difficult, but they are tolerated and seldom avoided.

When ready, the wedges are brought into the shop and cut into short lengths, approx. 1″ longer than the height of the *Kübel* to be made (ill. *c*). Each wedge is rived into several small billets (ill. *d*), using a froe and maul similar to those of a shingle maker (Fig. 157). Heartwood and any cracks or mold are removed. From one wedge are generally made two or three staves. A large number of staves ensure a round and stable *Kübel*. Enough are made so that after shaping, there is generally one extra piece to allow flexibility in assembly. Staves are trimmed with a short-handled broadax. They are cut to width and given a slight taper on the sides (ill. *e*).

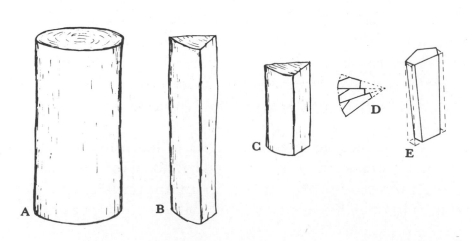

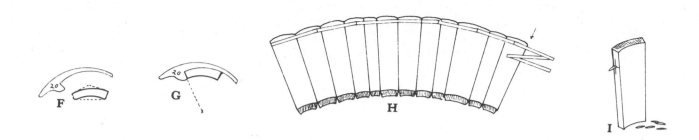

Work continues at a *Zugstuhl*, or "shaving horse," shown in Fig. 196. The principle is that the worker uses his feet to operate a swinging clamp, which is instantly adjustable. The force applied is very great due to leverage achieved by locating the fulcrum near the clamping head. Versions of shaving horses were formerly used by many craftsmen, including coopers, shingle makers, and others making tool handles, chair legs, slatted gates and fences, etc.

Tools used to finish out a rough stave are two drawknives, one flat and the other a convex hollowing knife. Using a drawknife requires strength and energy. The wood must be securely held, or it is pulled loose during work. With a very sharp drawknife, the skillful craftsman can quickly shape wood with great accuracy. Also necessary are a wooden breast bib (seen in Fig. 197) and an appropriate *Modell* (wooden pattern, ill. *f*, *g*) to which each stave is proportioned.

The upper convex half of a stave is made with the flat drawknife (Fig. 197). The stave is then turned around, and the lower half shaved to optically match the upper edge when viewed from the upper rim. A hollowing knife is used to scoop out the inside.

The next step is to bevel the stave edges. As seen in Fig. 198, the stave is held in place between the forward edge of the shaving horse and the breast bib. Fig. 199 depicts the writer finishing an edge on a jointer plane.

The work is next laid out for measurement on a work bench (ill. *h*). If the length equals the circumference desired within 2%, it is considered acceptable.

During assembly the *Kübel* is held together with stout wooden pegs fitted into holes in the stave edges (ill. *i*). These are cut from little blocks of yew, or slices of a stout conifer branch.

When the staves are fitted together one gets an idea of the size and shape of the *Kübel* being made (ill. *j*). From an assortment of riveted metal hoops, the *Küfer* selects one that will fit tightly near the lower rim of the *Kübel*. This is forced into place (ill. *k*) with a hammer and hoop driver. If the staves have been correctly made, they fit tightly, and the *Kübel* will already be strong.

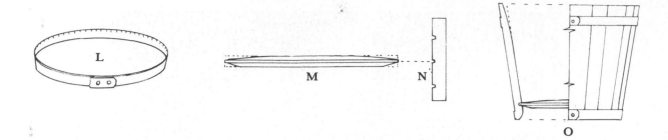

The end grain of the top rim is carefully moistened with a sponge, then planed smooth with a long jointer. The bottom rim must be sawn flat before it can be planed. Using a measure, four equal marks are made just beneath the rim. With a box saw, the *Küfer* aligns his cut by eye; the saw blade is kept parallel to the base of the *Kübel*—not perpendicular to the staves. The method is to saw round and round, ⅛″ deep with each pass. This results in a straight cut and a flat bottom edge. The rim is then planed.

Next is planing the interior. This is done with a set of small, specially curved wooden planes (Fig. 200), with soles ranging from almost flat to acutely crescent-shaped. A spoke shave is used to clean the outside surface.

Fig. 197–Shaping a *Kalberkübel* stave.

Fig. 198–Rough cutting an edge angle.

Making and fitting the permanent upper *Reifin* (hoop) follows. A length of galvanized steel strapping 1″ wide is cut to measurement. The strap is stretched along one side to fit the taper of the *Kübel* by means of blows from a square-headed hammer. The metal is bent into a hoop and held fast with two lead rivets. A crease is hammered into the overlap (ill. *l*), and the *Reifin* tried for size.

A *Fröscher* (English "croze"—a special cooper's tool) is used to groove the staves for holding the bottom. This tool (Fig. 200) is placed on the bottom rim and pushed round and round until a groove of proper depth is made. The bottom board is made of wood hewn from high quality pine. After being rived with a froe, it is smoothed at a shaving horse with a drawknife. Finally, the board is smoothed with a plane to a thickness of ¾″. A circle the size of the bottom is scribed on the board. One-sixth of the circumference, measured from within the groove, is used as a radius. This is cut with a band or bow saw. With a drawknife the edge is trimmed to the groove width (ill. *m*). Before fitting, the bottom edge is compressed with a slotted stick (ill. *n*), then sanded across the grain on both surfaces. Then the lower *Reifin* is removed and the bottom tapped in place (ill. *o*). With the *Reifin* back, about an ounce of water is put into the *Kübel* and swished around to swell the bottom joint.

Trimming and sanding are the last stages. A short-bladed knife is used to carve the inside of the bottom rim to form a neat "bull nose." A long-bladed knife is used for carving out the inside upper rim making a long, graceful taper. Finally, the *Kübel* is sanded.

The procedure described outlines steps I followed in making a plain round bucket with metal hoops. For three days I worked under Herr Kohler's guidance and patience. The finished *Kübel* was not particularly handsome, but I did learn a great deal about the theory and methods of the craft. Actually, it was not too homely, as the Meister had saved my awkward spoke shaving and interior planing, and I was a bit proud of this joint effort . . . until Herr Kohler took it out to the water trough for a test. Water leaked through the bottom, and it did not swell up. Back in the shop we measured the diameter at right angles and found a variation of three-sixteenths-inch. I watched the Meister take a brace and bit from the wall and proceed to drill six holes in the bottom. He then announced that this would make a fine garden planter.

For the remainder of the week I was put to work in the loft making fence posts out of a pile of seasoning pine limbs. These were cleaned of knots with a heavy brush hook, then skinned with a drawknife at a *Zugstuhl*. The large, energetic movements helped condition muscles (and calluses) and familiarize me with the tools. But I was alone, working in the loft, and so took occasional "rest stops" in the Meister's shop to observe his work in progress.

Short and stocky, Herr Kohler was a *Swingling* (alpine wrestling) champion in his youth. Now he uses the same force and energy in his craft. His strength is considerable and quite impressive to see when applied to wood. When he works with a drawknife, wood shavings fly into the air in all directions. I was intrigued by this use of physical strength combined with a great deal of accuracy.

FIG. 199–Planing an edge angle.

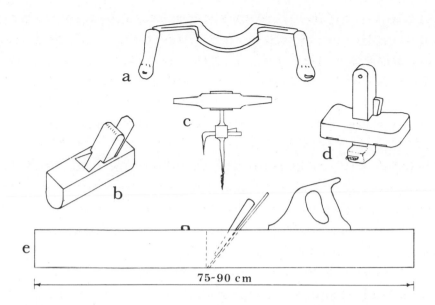

FIG. 200–Tools of the Swiss *Küfer* (a. hollowing drawknife; b. convex plane; c. adjustable auger; d. *Fröscher* ("croze"); e. jointer plane.)

At the end of this first week, Herr Kohler received a visit from an English speaking friend. For the first time since our arrival we were able to have a conversation with the Meister. When he understood that I was serious about an apprenticeship, he said that he had not expected to become a teacher, being used to the freedom of doing a wide variety of work. But after a few moments of reflection, he decided to try the experiment. Herr Kohler said that we would work Monday through Saturday, except on days when he had to work somewhere else on the mountain, and that I would eat noonday meals with the family. He said there was no need to make a written agreement, and that he had no money to pay me. This sounded strange, as I expected he might ask a fee. But the discussion turned to dinner, which was already on the table.

At precisely one o'clock the energetic octogenarian was busy riving wedges for *Kübelmachen*. A small stack of familiar looking staves was handed to me. In the preceding days I had thought about the first planter. I realized that using the special tools required a great deal of skill; accuracy, particularly in the bevel angles, is most important. I set to work with enthusiasm, determined to make a *Kübel* that would hold water. Work went somewhat easier than before, and I required less help from the Meister. The *Kübel* was still a three-day project. In fact, as I took on more complex work during the following months, I was never able to complete a piece in less time. Herr Kohler finished an average of one piece per day, depending on the project. He usually had three or four going at one time.

After sanding the *Kübel*, I checked it for roundness. The measurement was within 1 millimeter. I was ready for the water test, and Herr Kohler stopped his work on a milking bucket to examine my craftsmanship. Instead of going to the trough, he reached directly for his tool rack and removed the brace and bit. These he handed to me, indicating where to drill the drain holes! The check for leakage was never made; but I knew that this *was* a waterproof *Kübel*.

When I arrived the next morning, Herr Kohler had already prepared staves for my next project. This was a *Kalberkübel* (the large, oval-shaped bucket seen in Fig. 180). I was given two patterns: a small *Modell* used for making the side staves and a larger one for the two front pieces. The back, which includes the handle, is almost flat, and the shape is formed by eye. In all there were 15 staves.

I was happy to be making a *Kalberkübel*. Work progressed quite well, and the wood was better than had been used for making the planters (i.e., softer, less brittle, and straighter grain). The steps in construction are the same as already outlined, until coming to the bottom. A compass cannot very well measure an oval, so a different technique is adopted.

The high point in making a *Kalberkübel* comes in modeling the upper rim and curved handle. The rim is not flat, but gently bowed in the front, with a slight dip on either side. To make this, the rim is moistened, then carefully shaped with a very sharp drawknife. The handle is made with the same tool. To hold the work steady, the *Kalberkübel* is straddled with one leg over the rim. Work proceeds a little on each side until the graceful and symmetrical lines are finished. The hand hold is cut by scribing two parallel lines with a stout, short-bladed knife, then carving out the pulp until the blade emerges through the wood. A hole for hanging is bored with an auger (Fig. 200).

During the third week I made two other *Kalberkübel*. I began to get a feel for carving the handles, and could do most of the other steps with little help. I began to wonder what we would do with so many buckets, and so gave the best to Armin.

The Meister then put me to work making a small *Schussel*, a bowl 10″ in diameter, and 4″ deep. This was to be made using interlocked wooden *Reifin* (Fig. 202), a specialty of the Swiss *Küfer*. The first trick I learned was that temporary metal bands are needed in the early stages. Glue is also used. This is not permanent, but serves only to hold the *Schussel* together for spoke shaving and fitting the wooden *Reifin*. It was after five on a Saturday afternoon when glue was applied, and the metal bands driven onto the *Schussel* to act as tight clamps. After this I swept the shop, and returned to Chirel Alp for evening milking.

On Monday I expected to start making a wooden *Reifin*. But, to my surprise, Herr Kohler was finishing the piece I had been working on. At my place was a pile of staves for another *Schussel*. While at work I noticed that my *Kübel* were no longer in the corner. I inquired, and the Meister replied that they had been sold.

This revelation dissolved my daydreams, in which I already had my wares at our farm in America. I was suddenly reminded that I had entered into a semi-formal relationship. In this tradition, the apprentice works for the master; he is taught fundamental skills, which are put to use on the job. After the initial surprise, I was rather pleased that this work had brought some profit to Herr Kohler, as I had not even imagined there to be a market for it. Later, I learned that *Kalberkübel* are much sought after by alpine dairymen because they are seldom available. They take too much time to make for an object that cannot command an economically viable price. In the weeks that followed, I continued to help with Herr Kohler's work on various projects.

To make a wooden *Reifin* is the most difficult part of this work. The wood must be tough, yet easy to work. It should not expand or shrink under continual wetting and drying. Most commonly used is the trunk of a young maple tree that has grown quickly near a spring located in an open area. Only wood from below the first limb is usable. The grain must be straight, and there can be no cracks (caused by wind bending). Green wood (less than six months from cutting) is preferred; aged stock is acceptable but harder and more risky to work. Other usable woods are walnut, ash, and occasionally branches from conifer trees—although these tend to be brittle, and may suddenly split.

Knowing the difficulty of the work, I was hesitant to ask about making a wooden *Reifin*. However, I was anxious to try before my apprenticeship expired. I decided to request a project—an alpine milking bucket. This was met with a chuckle which continued through the morning. The Meister explained that a milking bucket would be "too risky." He said that the staves are thin, and no patterns are used in shaping them. The milking bucket, representing the peak of the *Küfer*'s craft, is made entirely by eye. I then offered an alternate—to make a *Schussel* with the sides carved out, such as on the milking bucket. This carving is ornamental, but it is also a functional necessity. The sides of a bucket must be tapered, in order that the hoops can be driven on tightly. But on a milking bucket it is advantageous to exaggerate this angle, making an enlarged lip for accepting the milk. The tapered sides also help hold the accumulating weight of the bucket between one's legs during milking. With the angle so obtuse, it would be impossible for the hoops to stay in place. An accommodation must be made; the solution is to carve an almost vertical seat for the hoops to fit into. Herr Kohler accepted my request; in fact, I had the opportunity to work on several wooden *Reifin* before leaving.

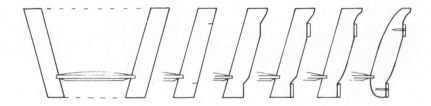

FIG. 201–Steps in finishing a bucket with curved staves.

I cannot say that I became a *Küfer*, nor was that my purpose. I did find the tradition of the craft to be a centering focus for a whole and integrated life. The *Küfer* follows his work from felling a tree to the completion of a functional object. The raw materials are local resources, and the *Küfer* supplies a local need. The involvement and cooperation among members of the community in which he lives and works is traditionally deep. The work is highly skilled and specialized, and gives him a basis for cash income or trade with his neighbors; but he is not limited to his craft as an "occupation." He is able to supply the demand working only part time. So the *Küfer* is also a farmer on the same level of involvement as the rest of the community, and self-sufficient as far as providing food and shelter for his family.

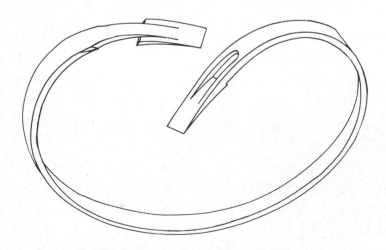

FIG. 202–Interlocking clasp of a wooden *Reifin*.

XVI. AFTERWORD

LOOKING back, as well as ahead, we see our year abroad as the beginning of a much longer journey. We left the United States with the intention of studying traditional rural architecture, feeling instinctively that these structures held generations of wisdom that may be of benefit to those seeking a healthy relationship with the earth today. We quickly discovered that we were not satisfied taking photographs of buildings, but wanted to know the people living inside these dwellings, and to learn about their lives. Thus the subject of *Handmade* expanded and we found ourselves apprenticed to our farmer and craftsmen hosts. We travelled, rather like journeymen, moving from shepherd to wheat farmer, cheese maker and cooper, until we knew it was time to put the pieces together and absorb what we had learned.

A year of writing has allowed us to travel even deeper into our experiences—to view them not as memories, but as valuable teachings and strong influences on our lives today. Perhaps most important is the affirmation of our belief in the *semi*-self-contained household unit, or homestead. In this situation the object of effort is not financial achievement, but a livelihood based on a use economy of working with indigenous resources in self-maintaining cycles. Thus life becomes an adventure of living with what *is*, rather than a state of fantasy where one is constantly dependant on manufactured products and the authority of "experts" on every subject.

Fig. 205–Bavaria.

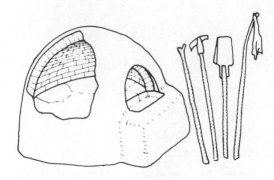

Fɪɢ. 206–Construction of typical bake oven with working implements. Greece.

Information and skills gleaned from rural householders formed the bulk of our material. But it is the rhythm and quality of life behind this history that we wish to develop as it is the subtler teachings that have made deeper impressions.

In many instances we found a consciousness of connection between people, work, and environment in the daily rhythm. Animals and fields were direct providers of sustenance and looked upon with love and gratitude. When we stayed with a Turkish farmer he showed us his home and fields with pride and went to his storeroom to share the harvest. We ate with the family and knew our food was the fruit of their labor. We felt the same closeness to the earth as we watched a Greek farmer lead his one cow to fresh pasture each day. In the evening he brought us a bottle of milk which tasted like the perfume of spring wild flowers. Family animals enjoy a similar intimate relationship in Switzerland, as evidenced by the hugs of welcome they received on their return home from the Alps. We sensed this intimacy between Herr Kohler and his wood working while hiking through the forest searching for a hard root twisted to the shape of a butter churn stand.

Sharing so many lifestyles with our many hosts convinced us that "the good life" has little to do with freeways, synthetics, or super-technology. We have found through experience, not argument, that being in direct contact with friends, gardens, tools and materials is the most healthful way to conduct our lives.

When the sun rises, I go to work,
When the sun goes down, I take my rest,
I dig the well from which I drink,
I farm the soil that yields my food,
I share creation, Kings can do no more.

—Ancient China, 2500 ʙ.ᴄ.

Annotated Bibliography

Daldy, A. F. *Small Buildings in Earthquake Areas.* Watford, England: Department of the Environment, 1972. [Valuable booklet for makers of small structures, costs 75p.]

Felders, Peter. *Das Aargauer Strohaus.* Bern, Switzerland: Verlag Paul Haupt, 1961. [Swiss thatching, text in German.]

Gotas, Harold B. *Composting.* Geneva: World Health Organization, 1956. [Sanitary disposal and reclamation of organic wastes, including methane digestors.]

Gschwend, Max. *Schweizer Bauernhäuser.* Bern, Switzerland: Verlag Paul Haupt, 1971. [Swiss farm houses shown in beautiful color plates and fine drawings.]

Howard, Sir Albert. *An Agricultural Testament.* Oxford: Oxford University Press, 1940. [Foundations of organic farming by the movement's first modern expositor.]

Jenkins, J. Geraint. *Traditional Country Craftsmen.* London: Routledge and Kegan Paul, 1956. [Chair bodging, wattle hurdle making, thatching, *et cetera*.]

King, F. H. *Farmers of Forty Centuries.* Emmaus, Penna.: Organic Gardening Press, 1973. [An agronomist's 1911 survey of permanent agriculture in China, Korea, and Japan; fascinating reading.]

Lappé, Francis M. *Diet For A Small Planet.* New York: Friends of the Earth and Ballantine Books, 1971. [You and Earth and protein.]

Merrill, Anthony F. *The Rammed-Earth House.* New York: Harper & Brothers, 1947. [Plain talk on use of mud, including a practical method of determining suitability of indigenous material.]

Morse, Edward S. *Japanese Homes and Their Surroundings.* New York: Dover Publications; Rutland, Vt.: Charles E. Tuttle Co. [Country and town houses of all classes, including methods of carpentry, reported in an account written before 1880.]

Nearing, Helen and Scott. *Living the Good Life.* New York: Schocken Books, 1954. [Practical information plus a solid discussion of cash vs. use economy; and the social importance of modern farmsteading.]

New Sources of Energy, Volume VII (Wind Power). New York: United Nations, 1961. [Verily, the oldest sources; proceedings from a United Nations conference in Rome.]

Reynolds, John. *Windmills and Waterwheels.* New York: Praeger Publishers. [Pictorial and historical material including floating mills, tide mills, use in textile production, iron hammering, aqueducts and drainage.]

Sturt, George. *The Wheelwright's Shop.* Cambridge: Cambridge University Press, 1923. [Valuable information for those involved in hand wood working—from selecting trees and seasoning wood to use of traditional tools.]

The Thatcher's Craft. Wimbledon, England: Rural Industries Bureau, 1961. [A complete text on thatching with hundreds of excellent photographs.]

Fig. 207–Plowing in Turkey.

Index of Recipes